DISCOVER YOUR SWEET SPOT

"I only read and endorse books by people who are the living proof of their message. Scott Fay is certainly a man who has found and lives in his Sweet Spot. Read this book and he can help you discover and live in yours too."

—**Darren Hardy**, Publisher *SUCCESS*, CEO Mentor and
N.Y. Times Best Selling Author of *The Compound Effect.*

Scott's words challenge us to consider a new way of thinking and then equip us to take that journey ourselves.

—**Kevin Hall**, Author of *Aspire.*
Business Consultant, Speaker, and Coach

"Scott Fay is both one of the wisest and kindest human beings I have the privilege to know. If you can imagine the combination of a phenomenal amount of life and business wisdom with a heart as big as the state in which he resides (and, it's a big state), then you now know you have the opportunity to embark on a journey that will add immense value, joy and richness to your life, as well as to the lives of those you touch. Follow the the 7 proven steps he reveals and you will find yourself living in that place where your purpose, your passion and your plan intersect. In other words, you'll *Discover Your Sweet Spot.*"

—**Bob Burg**, coauthor of *The Go-Giver*

For over a decade I have had a front row seat of watching Scott Fay discover and live from his Sweet Spot. Now with this book, you too can learn, laugh, and be challenged from the real and incredible stories of perseverance, failure, triumph and a walk of faith few get to witness. I'm grateful I had the chance to see the stories unfold live through our friendship, and you will be grateful that you have read the book.

—**Paul Martinelli**, Internationally Acclaimed
Speaker, Trainer, and Coach

A masterful model of transformation. Scott's examples from all sectors of society make this a dynamic read.

—**John Ruhlin**, #1 All Time Cutco Distributor out of 1 Million+

It was 10 years ago that the Author of this book helped me discover my Sweet Spot. Since then, I was able to transform my business from a small local business, into the world leader in our space growing my business by 4,300%. In a day when many talk about the value of "getting you out of your comfort zone", Scott will help you discover the transforming power of *Discovering Your Sweet Spot.*

—**James Crocker**, President & CEO of Waterblasting Technologies

My prediction: Literary critics and book reviewers will enthusiastically commend, hail, and applaud this latest writing, so that *Discover Your Sweet Spot* will accelerate to the top-ten list of books.

—**Tom Feltenstein**, Best-selling Author and President & CEO of Power Marketing Academy

As you read *Discover Your Sweet Spot*, you will find explosive ideas on how to practically and professionally build success. Scott Fay gets it!

—**Dr. Mark A. Smith**, President, Ohio Christian University

DISCOVER YOUR SWEET SPOT

The 7 Steps to Create a Life of Success and Significance

SCOTT M. FAY

NEW YORK

DISCOVER YOUR SWEET SPOT
The 7 Steps to Create a Life of Success and Significance

Published in New York, New York, by Morgan James Publishing. Morgan James and The Entrepreneurial Publisher are trademarks of Morgan James, LLC.
www.MorganJamesPublishing.com

The Morgan James Speakers Group can bring authors to your live event. For more information or to book an event visit The Morgan James Speakers Group at www.TheMorganJamesSpeakersGroup.com.

Published in association with Kary Oberbrunner
Redeem the Day, P.O. Box 43 Powell, OH, 43065, www.karyoberbrunner.com

ISBN 978-1-61448-592-6 paperback
ISBN 978-1-61448-593-3 eBook
ISBN 978-1-61448-594-0 audio
ISBN 978-1-63047-029-6 hard cover
Library of Congress Control Number:
2013933437

Cover Design by:
Rachel Lopez
www.r2cdesign.com

Interior Design by:
Bonnie Bushman
bonnie@caboodlegraphics.com

For my three kids—Debby, Andrew, and Jessica—who quite possibly taught me more than anyone else.

For Debby:

You taught me so many lessons about the love between a child and a father—like the time your affection prepared me to receive a significant gift. You taught me that Our Heavenly Father is incredibly generous and exceptionally kind.

For Andrew:

You taught me so many lessons about friendship—like the time we took a four-day, 1000-mile snowmobile trek through the Michigan wilderness. You taught me that loving includes laughing right through the snow, the wrecks, and the low visibility.

For Jessica "Sugg" (pronounced "shug" as in "sugar"):

You taught me so many lessons about the sweetness of life—like the time we took our daddy/daughter trip to Chicago. You taught me the wisdom of touring a luxury car dealership before we hit the Magnificent Mile for clothing shopping. (Smart girl.)

TABLE OF CONTENTS

FOREWORD

My name is John and I'm your friend. And because I'm your friend I must tell you something important.

As can be expected, there's good news and bad news.

But perhaps unexpectedly, there's *even more* good news.

First the good news. You have a sweet spot.

The bad news? Few people know their sweet spot.

But the *other* good news? You're holding in your hands a very important tool in helping you discover your sweet spot.

My good friend, Scott Fay, discovered his sweet spot years ago and when he did, his life drastically changed. Finding his place and staying there set him on a course where he soon found success *and* significance. Decades later, he's still living within that sweet spot and, as a result, he's still tasting success *and* significance.

I often say successful people discover their strengths but successful leaders help others find the place where they will perform well. That's what Scott has done in this book.

He learned this transformational content from laying sod, not from sitting in school. He unearthed these seven proven steps with intentional effort, not casual commitment.

William James said, "You cannot travel without until you have travelled within." Socrates said, "The unexamined life is not worth living." People who discover their sweet spot are people who take the inward journey and examine themselves. They make the choice to live until they die.

My guess is you want this, too. If so, Scott will be your tour guide. He'll show you his successes *and* his setbacks. What qualifies him are his victories and—most important—what he learned from his defeats. So, I encourage you: get ready to dig deep and discover your sweet spot. I promise you, you'll love what you find.

John C. Maxwell

ACKNOWLEDGEMENTS

For Kary Oberbrunner.

You found the words to describe the story inside my head.

For Tom Balling.

You allowed me to focus in my sweet spot and subsequently took our services and construction companies to a completely new level.

For Paul Martinelli.

Your navigation and trust in our joint projects and businesses have opened up opportunities beyond my wildest imagination.

For Petra Crosier.

You were an excellent assistant through the process.

For my cousin, Dr. Wendy Pogozelski.

You gave the manuscript a final rinse.

For Stephan Seyfert.
You graciously gave this project an extra set of eyes.

For Dad and Mom.
You placed me in a leadership environment
from my earliest recollection.

For John C. Maxwell.
You mentored me from afar during the
first season of my life and up close ever since.

For my wife, Katherine.
You have given me an unbelievable gift of support and
shared with me in the belief that the best things in life take time.

A NOTE TO THE READER

A fancy New York magazine recently wrote an article about cologne. It said, "A man's scent of choice should smell like his personality."[1]

I tend to agree.

Ironically, I prefer the scent of diesel fuel mixed with dirt—not a personal choice based on how it smells, but rather what it represents.

Rest easy. I abstain from applying this scent when I'm on stage speaking to a group of leaders or entrepreneurs. Yet, those who know me best know that my preferred scent comes from my love for landscaping.

Whether or not you're a fan of landscaping, a closer look at diesel fuel and dirt reveal truths related to personal growth, leadership development, and organizational health. During the last few decades, I've been able to convert these truths into what I call The Sweet Spot System ™. By utilizing this system within my life and my businesses, I've been able to achieve incredible results.

Imagine if you discovered how The Sweet Spot System™ could work for you. Imagine if you used the seven proven steps to create the life you want. What results would you experience? Better finances? Better focus? Better relationships?

This system equipped me to do all three and much more. Specifically, The Sweet Spot System™ helped me acquire fourteen distressed businesses and turn them into profitable environments for leadership and commerce. It prepared me to forge a partnership with the number one leadership guru in the world, John C. Maxwell, and create the world's fastest growing speaking, coaching, and training team with Paul Martinelli. It primed me to start several other ventures, projects, and initiatives related to my core strengths. Finally, it enabled me to create a robust life filled with a variety of activities including regular snowmobiling in Michigan and walks on the Florida beaches with my wife, Katherine, all in the same week.

If this system can work for me—a guy who wears jeans and boots and drives a pickup truck—then be encouraged: it can work you, too. In fact, it can work for any individual or organization serious about creating a growth environment. It centers around three concepts every landscaper understands: design, build, and maintain.

So if you're ready to dig into The Sweet Spot System™ and experience its amazing potential, then hop into my pickup truck and get ready for an adventure.

Our story begins with, of all things, grape bubble gum.

INTRODUCTION:
SON OF A PREACHER MAN

Grape bubble gum changed my life.

Well, maybe put more accurately, grape bubble gum changed *the course* of my life.

Here's the story. In fourth grade, I became a businessman. If you're tempted to be impressed, don't be. I'm not that strategic. No, my little economical enterprise ignited by accident.

One ordinary morning, I stood waiting at my school bus stop, looking for anything *but* a yellow school bus. Mildly entertained by stepping on and off the curb, I impatiently fidgeted. Anyone could have seen that a cowboy would have had better luck taming an ornery bull than attempting to make me stand still.

While aimlessly pacing, I looked down at the ground and caught a glimpse of something shiny. Like a shark smelling blood, I quickly secured my prize. Further inspection revealed a treasure worth keeping. Or, on second thought, maybe a treasure worth spending.

This shiny quarter would be my ticket to a treat at Killenberger's Grocery Store in East Worcester, New York. The son of a preacher man, I grew up between the towns of Oneonta and Cobleskill, alongside a trucking route that proudly boasted one solitary stoplight in the whole town. The stoplight even blinked. And if *you* blinked on Route 7, you'd miss the entire town. No matter. We didn't mind our humble beginnings. We grew up poor, and best of all, we didn't even know it. My dad's salary from the church he pastored was $45 a week and all the milk we could drink. Many of the parishioners owned small farms with 30–50 Holstein cows and they found pleasure in sharing milk and extra-tough beef with the pastor and his family.

Across from the grocery store stood our center of commerce: a fire station, Joe's Barber Shop, and the post office.

Although I enjoyed all three of those entities, on the day I discovered the quarter, I knew I was destined for greater geography—like the candy aisle in the grocery store. The little bell sounded my entrance and the old creaking wood floors announced my arrival. I waltzed in, financially confident and equipped in arithmetic, knowing that 25 cents could score me twenty-five individually wrapped pieces of grape bubble gum.

Although I normally enjoyed teasing my taste buds, on that particular day I exerted some form of self-control and only purchased five pieces—"one for now and four for later." The remaining 20 cents jingled in my pocket, alerting my classmates that a man with money had just entered their presence.

The school day dragged on slowly, like every other day, and by about 10:00 a.m. I was hungry and bored—not a good combination for a squirmy fourth-grade boy. But as fate would have it, this day I would discover my divine destiny.

In the middle of a lesson from our teacher, I reached in my pocket and felt the solution to boredom and hunger: four grape gum balls all wrapped up and ready to go. Instinctively, I pulled one out and, ignoring the crinkling wrapper that delivered a distraction to fellow classmates, I popped it in my mouth.

Immediately, the scent of artificial grape hijacked the room. One of the boys next to me shot a request in my direction, "Hey, Fay, give me one of those gum balls."

Without a second thought, I positioned a strategic up-sell. "Give me a nickel and it's yours," I replied back. And with that transaction so began my grape bubble gum business.

I quickly discovered laws about pricing, supply and demand, marketing, and word of mouth advertising.

While this is a true story, you know fourth-grade boys eventually grow up. Most transition out of the grape gum ball businesses and into something with a little more bite. And so, at 12 years old, I sunk my teeth into starting a grass-cutting and landscape business that grew big enough that I could sell it six years later when I graduated from high school.

I took that hunger for business with me when I went to college. Some of my buddies drove onto the south Florida campus in sports cars. Always the outlier, I showed up two weeks before the semester started in a pick-up truck looking for grass (the type you cut, not the type you smoke).

During the next few years, I learned leadership and business principles out of necessity. Although just a teenager myself, I eventually employed a staff of twenty-four, including many fellow students. Profits from the landscaping business paid for my college tuition.

After graduating from college, getting married, and then selling the business, my journey led me back to New York for a time and then back to Hobe Sound, Florida, again where I still do what I love today: landscaping. But my journey hasn't always been bright. I've had my fair share of failures. I know what qualifies me to share with you is not my success but my setbacks. In the past, I've lost money and momentum, but I've learned some amazing principles along the way. In fact, seven principles have helped me be more, do more, have more, and give more. These seven proven steps form The Sweet Spot System™.

In the following chapters, we'll explore these steps one at a time. But for now, here's a peek at the system, just so you have a complete picture.

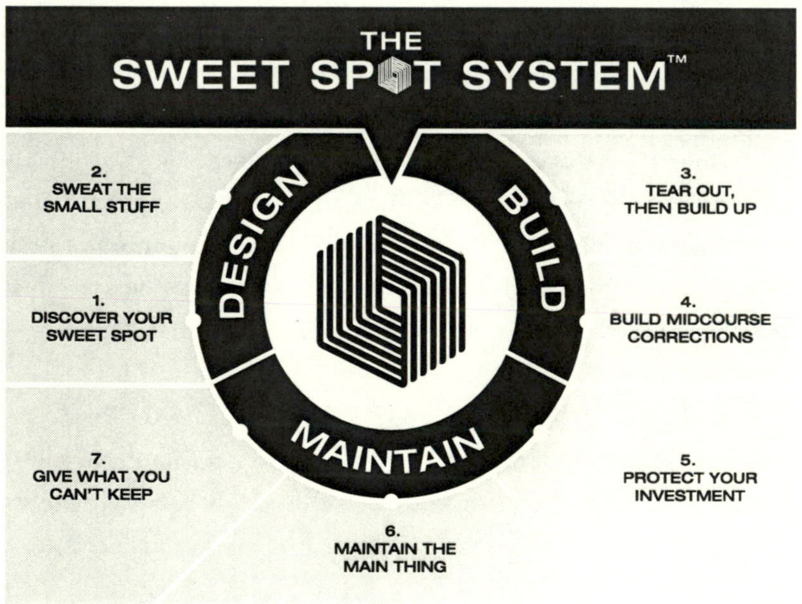

Recently, I've been given the opportunity to share this system with other individuals and organizations and see them achieve their goals. Regardless of the audience, I always start with the topic of environment first.

Here's what I know.

In order to build my organizations, I first needed to build myself. And in order to build myself, I needed to create an environment conducive to my growth.

Think about it. As humans, space is essential. For starters, we take up space. But more than that, we also design space, build space, and even maintain space. In landscaping, we intentionally utilize space with a specific purpose in mind. But too often when leading ourselves and those around us, we unintentionally permit a space that sabotages our potential.

I've never met people who felt they achieved their full potential. This tells me that we're all living and leading below our capacity. Imagine what we could do if we were just a few percentage points better. Imagine what we could create or accomplish.

When we look to nature, we can see a powerful and encouraging example. Think about an acorn for a moment. It possesses tremendous potential. As the fourteenth century proverb teaches, "Great oaks from little acorns grow."

But if we place an acorn in a safe, comfortable, and protected place, we will watch it slowly die over time. In these types of environments, acorns will do nothing. Yet if we take this same acorn and stick it in the ground, something miraculous happens. This little acorn sends out a powerful signal to the surrounding soil. It attracts everything it needs in order to grow and thrive.

The acorn doesn't need a safe, comfortable, and protected place. It needs a conducive environment to unleash its potential. And when it grows, it increases in size and strength, but also in productivity. This same acorn—now a mighty oak—produces other acorns.

The average oak tree produces 70,000–150,000 acorns a year. During the tree's entire life, that number jumps to around 13.5 million acorns.[2] And this staggering number doesn't even account for the other acorns that will come from that first acorn's acorns and so on.

The next time you hold an acorn, realize the potential of 13.5 million other acorns coming from the one in your hand—all conditional upon its environment.

American author Ken Kesey wisely observed, "We can count how many seeds are in the apple, but not how many apples are in the seed."

Similarly, you can't measure your potential either. In an environment conducive to growth, you'll increase in strength and multiply your impact, too.

I believe you're already successful or you wouldn't be reading this book. But imagine if you got better. Imagine if you had all the resources and belief you needed to reach your potential. Imagine if you were planted in an environment that propelled you further instead of one that held you back.

These types of environments do exist. Chick-fil-A attracts high-level leaders because of the environment it designs, builds, and maintains. Recently, 22,000 people applied to become owner/operators of Chick-fil-A restaurants. That's not impressive until you learn that these 22,000 people were competing for ninety positions. Hopefuls flock to Chick-fil-A in order to be part of its environment.

The president and chief operating officer of Chick-fil-A, Dan Cathy, intentionally creates a leadership environment that breeds loyalty and results. Because the restaurant has a lot to lose if it hires the wrong employee, its leaders create a very clear selection strategy. Applicants are evaluated on competence, character, and chemistry.[3] Chick-fil-A managers know that if they hire the wrong people, they'll threaten their environment.

Forbes magazine, among many other publications, noticed this environment and published an enlightening article a few years back titled "The Cult of Chick-fil-A". In the article, author Emily Schmall quoted Cathy as saying, "The turnover among Chick-fil-A operators is a low 5% a year. We tell applicants, 'If you don't intend to be here for life, you needn't apply,'."

Dan Cathy is following in his father's footsteps, implementing a vision that positions Chick-fil-A in the people business serving chicken sandwiches rather than the chicken sandwich business serving people. By creating this intentional environment, Dan Cathy is also creating influence and income.

We have choices.

We can create environments by accident or by intention. In the landscaping business, I've witnessed some pretty ugly environments. These particular land owners didn't try to make their properties unattractive. The truth is they didn't *try* to do anything. And that's the problem. Hoping for an effective environment is a great goal, but hope isn't a strategy.

Regardless of your current situation, I believe you're meant for more. But I also believe your growth won't happen by accident.

In landscaping, we use a three-fold strategy to ensure a beautiful environment: the design phase, the build phase, and the maintain phase.

On our journey through this book, we'll follow a similar strategy. In our first phase, we'll encounter the power and potential of intentionally designing an environment conducive to leadership. In our second phase, we'll discover practical skills and strategies to help build a desired leadership environment for ourselves and our organizations. And in the final phase, we'll learn effective tools that equip us to maintain our leadership environment to ensure a lasting personal and organizational legacy.

Don't get too serious, though. The environments I create tend to be inviting and practical and so is this book. We might even laugh a little along the way. I'm excited to share initiatives I'm currently using which are helping my organization take huge leaps forward. Initiatives like: "I Love My Job" and "Just Say it Once".

I'm honored to take this adventure with you and I'm committed to your success. I'll leverage whatever I can to help you grow.

At this point in our relationship, if you were in my office in sunny Hobe Sound, Florida, I'd pass you the bowl full of crinkly wrapped grape bubble gum and offer you a piece. Unfortunately, I couldn't convince my publisher to comply. No worries. I'll pop one in my mouth for you and let the scent fill my office.

Get ready to begin designing. I promise we'll have some fun along the way.

PHASE 1:

DESIGN YOUR LEADERSHIP ENVIRONMENT

STEP 1:

DISCOVER YOUR SWEET SPOT

Design with the End in Mind

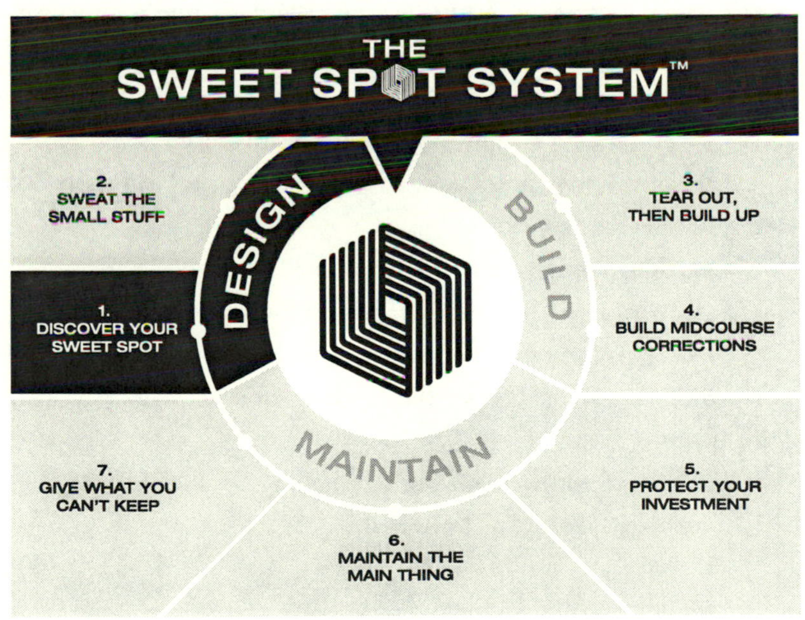

"What do you plan on doing with the new space?" I inquired with genuine interest.

You'd be surprised how few of my clients know the answer to this question.

"I'm not sure I know what you're asking," he responded back with equal sincerity. "I thought you were just going to pick out some good-looking trees and shrubs for us. You're the professional. Isn't that why we hired your team?"

"I'm definitely up for advising you along the way," I said reassuringly. "But trust me, designing with the end in mind will help tremendously. Think about it this way: as you imagine the new space we're designing for you, what do you see yourself doing in that space? Are you hosting garden parties with friends? Do you see yourself sitting next to a small waterfall feature in the evenings while reading your favorite novel? Or maybe you picture your grandkids playing Frisbee with you in the backyard on a plush green lawn?"

A warm smile slowly spread across my client's face.

"OK, I get it now. You know, come to think of it, I can see myself doing all three!" he chuckled.

"One thing though, Scott," he shot back.

"Sure, what is it?" By this time, I anticipated a little humor.

"Before I give you my final answer, I just have to ask...do you have any additional options besides those three? After all, I don't want to limit any fun."

At this comment, we both started laughing.

"Now you're getting it," I grinned.

I start every job the same way, helping my clients design with the end in mind.

It's always better to talk through their desires in the design phase than to work them out in the build phase. Designing with the end in mind saves them money and it saves me time. Although my landscaping team is always happy to help, and we can do almost anything, most clients don't have an endless supply of money. A little intentional thinking on the front end saves everyone time and money on the back end.

But this principle reaches far beyond waterfalls and flowerbeds. In fact, it touches every single one of us. Although we might not be able to literally design the environment around us, we're each given the responsibility to design a conducive environment within us.

Effective and efficient leaders embody this type of healthy space. Unfortunately, this space is highly uncommon and only reflective of those who function within their Sweet Spot. Perhaps you've heard about the Sweet Spot in other contexts—like baseball, for example. If a batter hits the ball on the Sweet Spot of the bat, he doesn't even need to look to see if he hit the ball over the fence. He just intuitively knows.

But more significant than baseball, we each have the potential for a Sweet Spot in our lives. I define the Sweet Spot as the convergence of three things: Purpose, Passion, and Plan.

Purpose is who you are designed to *be*.

Passion is what you love to *do*.

Plan is the *strategic convergence* of being and doing.

I explain the Sweet Spot like this:

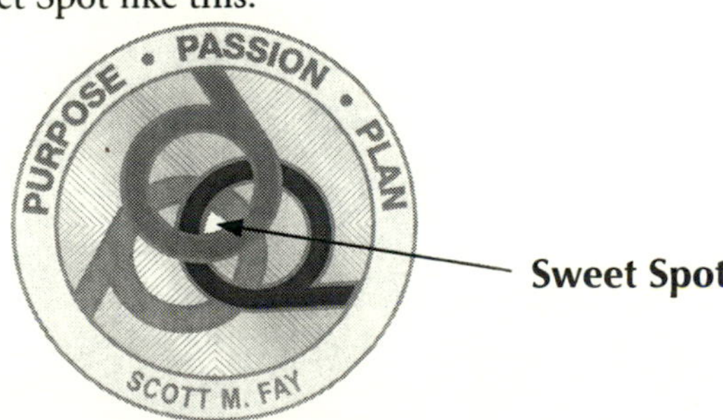

Living and working from our Sweet Spot results from intentional design, not accidental disorder. Similar to what I do with my new landscaping clients, we must design our lives with the end in mind. Unfortunately, too many people just accept their lives rather than *lead* their lives.

The price of life outside our Sweet Spot proves costly. Our work feels like toil and we spend our energy moving sideways instead of forward. We're not effective and therefore neither are the environments that we create.

But the opposite is true as well. Living to and from our Sweet Spot yields exponential potential.

My mother still tells me that I first found my Sweet Spot at the age of four while playing in the sandbox. Every day in summer, I loved spending time in a gigantic 10-by 15-foot sandpit with toy 'dozers, trailers, and trucks. Like boys my age, I built roads and rivers during playtime. But perhaps unlike other boys, I also built little homes out of sand and then I felt the need to landscape those little properties. I'd use pine cones for shrubs, twigs for trees, and place little stones around freshly-dug miniature swimming pools.

In that vast sand pit, I made a little square shop out of red bricks that I'd found lying around from my father's projects. On top of that square shop, I made a flat roof out of pine boards.

I'd spend nearly all day playing in the sand pit. But just before dinnertime, I'd perform a unique ritual. I'd drive the equipment up onto the trailers, hook them up to the trucks, and then drive the trucks back to the square shop with the flat roof. By this time, mom would make a final dinner call and, according to her, I'd spend a couple more minutes at the shop off-loading the equipment, lining up the trailers, and, finally, backing up the trucks. Ritual complete, I'd head off to dinner, satisfied and smiling.

What about you? Have you ever functioned in your Sweet Spot? Do you know what it is? Is your Passion, Purpose, and Plan clear?

If so, then just like the baseball example, you don't even need to look to see if you're effective. You already know.

Although I haven't always functioned in my Sweet Spot, I've come pretty close.

Regretfully, though, I remember one specific season when I fell out of my Sweet Spot. The price for my mistake proved expensive and I felt like a duck out of water. I almost destroyed my young family financially, not to mention emotionally and relationally as well.

Here's the quick story. Just after I completed college, my dad lost one of his associates. In order to help him in his pinch, I sold the landscaping business in Florida and moved the family up to New York so I could enter the ministry with him. After a couple weeks, I knew I made the wrong choice so I gave a six-month notice of my resignation. To make matters worse, I exchanged one bad decision for half a dozen more. I ended up laboring at six different jobs in three and a half years, including selling life insurance, supplying copiers and fax machines, and operating vending machines and arcade games.

In those years, work felt like work because I wasn't functioning in my calling. I sank like a tank because I left my love of landscaping. I wasn't engaged in the work, so the environments I created in those years weren't engaging either.

Thankfully, today I have a tremendous team around me that helps me stay in my Sweet Spot. These talented people know I'm most effective and productive when I focus on the convergence of my three circles: Purpose, Passion, and Plan.

My mentor, John Maxwell, shed some more light on the subject by teaching me to answer three critical questions related to the Sweet Spot:

- What is required of me?
- What yields the highest return?
- What creates the greatest reward?

I work hard at answering these three questions every day. And when I feel myself getting out of alignment, then I adjust. Reflecting and planning help bring clarity.

More than forty years later, I still perform an odd ritual. Today my sandpit is a bit larger, though. On most days before dinnertime, I pull into a square shop with a flat roof at 7900 SE Bridge Road in Hobe Sound, Florida. While driving around the lot, I see my employees off-loading the equipment, lining up the trailers, and, finally, backing up the trucks. Waving to them, I see the ritual completed and then I head off to dinner satisfied and smiling.

Because I'm fully engaged in work and life, I naturally create engaging environments wherever I go. Sometimes these environments are in the sandpit and sometimes they're on the stage. Regardless, I still feel like that four-year-old kid having a blast. And even when I'm supposed to be working, I feel like I'm playing, all because I've discovered my Sweet Spot. I'm on my way to becoming what philosopher L. P. Jacks calls, "a master in the art of living." Here's his compelling observation:

> *A master in the art of living draws no sharp distinction between his work and his play; his labor and his leisure; his mind and his body; his education and his recreation. He hardly knows which is which. He simply pursues his vision of excellence through whatever he is doing, and leaves others to determine whether he is working or playing. To himself, he always appears to be doing both.*[4]

By living in the light of our Sweet Spot and managing our internal environment better, we increase our external influence on those around us.

The other day someone asked me if I knew what the words *influence* and *influenza* had in common. Feeling like a contestant on the TV show *Are You Smarter Than a 5th Grader*, I admitted my ignorance. The gentleman willingly gave the answer, "Both influence and influenza are incredibly contagious."

These two words share the same root word and both are often transmitted very easily. Although there are exceptions, most people get sick when they're exposed to a strong strain of influenza. Ironically, most people get better when they're exposed to a strong leader who creates a healthy environment. Like attitudes, environments are contagious. And both begin with the individual before they seep into the organization.

But beware. These environmental laws are no respecter of persons. They simply reflect and magnify what's already inside the individual. If a person is negative, then he or she is naturally predisposed to create a negative environment.

Disengaged individuals consciously or subconsciously create disengaged environments. Nature works against those who think otherwise and nature weeds out hypocrisy, regardless of the best intentions.

Thankfully, engaged people create engaging environments. Engaged people make it easier for the people around them to get better. Engaged people have influence and influence is contagious.

Recent history provides a few compelling examples of individuals who discovered their Sweet Spot and allowed their internal environment to influence their external one.

Former Detroit Lions running back Barry Sanders showed us how to excel as an undersized running back despite playing for a rather mediocre team. Holocaust survivor Viktor Frankl modeled how to overcome incredible obstacles by identifying purpose in pain. And political prisoner Nelson Mandela taught us greatness can't be caged.

In all of these examples, we see people who first created a conducive environment within themselves. As a result, their unhealthy external environment didn't destroy their healthy internal one. Impressively, the internal environment they designed, built, and maintained proved so strong and so well-defined that it helped them transform their external one.

Barry's moves mesmerized us.

Viktor's reflections equipped us.

And Nelson's resolve won the day.

Our attitude directly determines the results we get. By examining these truths, we bump up against an important leadership law. The environment we long to express "out there" must first be created "in here."

Each of these individuals discovered his Sweet Spot and took personal responsibility for his internal environment. Only then could he cultivate the potential to change his external one. We can't give away what we don't have ourselves, and we can't export what we don't already possess.

Barry couldn't perform if he let his external environment deter him.

Viktor couldn't survive if he let his external environment destroy him.

Nelson couldn't flourish if he let his external environment discourage him.

Interestingly, these people designed their internal environment long before they became famous. Barry designed an internal competitive mindset in his early football days at Wichita North High School. Viktor Frankl designed an internal emotional and psychological intelligence during his studies at the University of Vienna and his residency at the Steinhof Psychiatric Hospital. Nelson Mandela designed fierce mental resolve at the University of Fort Hare while serving on the Student Representative Council. These three leaders prepared for their moment from an early age and as a result their moment was prepared for them. They found their Sweet Spot and functioned from their Sweet Spot.

The people near Barry, Viktor, and Nelson observed their inner strength and faced a choice. They could choose to join them and embrace their environment or they could ignore them and reject their environment.

And so, in Chapter 1 we've come to discover that change always begins with us. By managing ourselves better we increase our potential to influence our environment and transform it for the better. We don't get what we want; we get who we are, and who we are flows directly back to our design.

As we close out this chapter, perhaps you'll humor me for a moment. I'd like to ask you what I ask all my new landscaping clients: "What do you plan on doing with the new space you want to create?" Or, perhaps even a little more relevant to our context, "Have you designed your life with the end in mind, in the light of your Sweet Spot?"

How you answer this question has significant bearing on the environment you'll inevitably create. Because what we design directly affects what we build.

STEP 2:

SWEAT THE SMALL STUFF

The Devils are in the Design

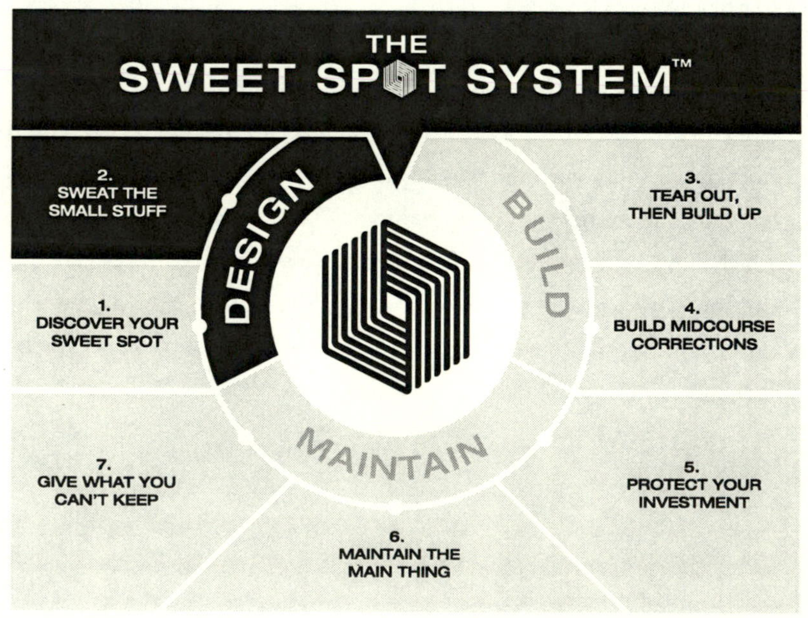

"Tracey, how are things going today?" I asked, pushing open the front door to the square shop with the flat roof.

"Oh, you know, Scott…it's a typical Monday morning," she shot back with a bit of a flustered tone.

"Uhhh, no Tracey, I don't know what you mean. Is there anything I can do to help?" I offered back.

"We have 170 people running around the yard. And everything that could go wrong, has gone wrong," she shared freely.

"And this is *typical*?" As CEO, I knew I couldn't let it go.

"Well, yeah. This is how Mondays always go. It's just another typical one," she replied and then went back to typing on her computer.

I measured my words carefully. "Tracey, I have to ask. How long have you been in this industry?"

"Twenty years," she shot back.

"And how many Mondays are there in an average year?" I paused so we could both let the answer sink in.

"Umm…about fifty," she replied.

"So if my math is correct, then you've had about 1,000 Mondays in your career?" I spoke slowly, wanting her to really get this."Yessssss… and…?" she responded impatiently. At this point I could tell she wanted the bottom line so I gave it to her.

"…and you've never tried to change the way your typical Mondays go?" I sincerely inquired.

"What do you mean?" she asked.

"Tracey, how many times do we have to trip on something before we pick it up? If a typical Monday means everything goes wrong, then how can we make it right?" I wanted to problem solve with her.

"I see your point," she verbalized with her new awareness. A fan of efficiency, she continued with a twinge of excitement, "Maybe we could change some things so that a new typical Monday would mean things go smoothly."

"Excellent," I complimented. "Why don't you make a list of what typically goes wrong so we can use that to design a better Monday? Then we can engage the team and implement some tweaks for the organization. Sound good?" I asked before heading to my office.

"Right on," Tracey replied while pulling a steno pad from one of her drawers. "I'll start immediately."

With a smile I opened my office door and let out a sigh of relief. Together, Tracey and I just identified and confronted one of the most toxic enemies of conducive environments: Design Devils.

You've probably heard the old adage, "The devil is in the details." Although this statement might contain some truth, within our conversation of creating conducive environments, we've tweaked the adage. We believe the devils are in the design.

It's too easy to simply blame results. Average individuals and organizations do this blaming and, unconsciously, this was Tracey's mindset, too. She expected her "typical Mondays" because she experienced 1,000 of them before. Without exception, things went wrong and Tracey was caught in a blame game with the results. They simply confirmed what she already planned with her design.

Snapping out of this cycle is easier said than done. It's often difficult because beliefs are forged slowly over time and they become part of us. But rest assured—change is possible.

On that particular day, I helped Tracey experience change by helping her overcome her Design Devils. I led her down a process I call the Five Devil Destroyers.

Here they are: I interrupted her story, challenged her beliefs, invited her evaluation, engaged her adjustments, and implemented her changes. Unpacking these one at a time will provide even more clarity.

1. **I interrupted her story.** We all have a story playing inside our heads, continuously, 24 hours a day, seven days a week. We rarely bother to interrupt this story. And if we're not aware, then today is simply a result of yesterday's recycled thinking. Unless we interrupt our story, tomorrow isn't looking any brighter either.
2. **I challenged her beliefs.** Only after we interrupt our story can we challenge our beliefs. Once we do, we often find some of our beliefs are based on myths. Other are just faulty. By questioning our beliefs, we test their quality. If our beliefs pass the test, we should keep them, but if not, we should reject them.
3. **I invited her evaluation.** Nothing empowers people like sincerely asking for their evaluation. Naturally, our brains enjoy relieving tension by solving problems. When we show people that we care enough to hear their perspective on a topic, most people are willing to share their feedback.
4. **I engaged her adjustments.** Just because people give their opinions doesn't mean they're valid. I've found dialoging around ideas helps me understand the beliefs behind them. Usually there's a reason for their rationale, and slowing down long enough to hear helps everyone who's involved.
5. **I implemented her changes.** The new ideas that remain do so for a reason. Although they're usually different then our original predictions, this is what makes the experience so powerful. Once the Design Devils are exposed, only then can they be redesigned.

Our typical Mondays changed because Tracey changed from focusing on the results to the design. She realized that before we can *build* the proper environment we must first *design* the proper environment.

It's been said that your life is getting the exact results it's *designed* to get. This is true about your business as well. We can curse the results, but unless we evaluate the design, we can't blame anybody but ourselves.

Sometimes a design should remain constant. Other times, in order to increase productivity and efficiency, designs should be reevaluated and then readjusted. Throughout history, breakthroughs occurred when Design Devils were challenged. We see this strategy in the epic legacies left by Steve Jobs with Apple and Jack Welch with GE. Both men approached their roles with a firm resolve to discover the Design Devils. Once they found them, they made sure to employ the Five Devil Destroyers. These leaders interrupted the story, challenged the beliefs, invited the evaluation, engaged the adjustments, and implemented the changes.

In both companies, the stakes were high. Yet, both leaders intuitively knew that unless they changed their design, they didn't have a chance at changing their results.

In April 1981, 45-year-old Jack Welch became the CEO and chairman of General Electric, the tenth best company on the stock market. The company was ninety years old and worth about $12 billon at this time. With each decade, GE had acquired additional businesses and by 1981, the number of acquired businesses reached 350.

All was not well, though. The U.S. found itself in a recession with high interest rates and suffered from the highest unemployment rates since the Depression. Most CEOs would have found comfort in the diversified business model, but not Welch. Instead, he saw Design Devils that held GE back. Believing in a better design, he went to work on what he called "the hardware revolution".

Almost immediately, Welch redesigned the environment. He set the standard for each business to become the number one or two competitor in its industry—or to disengage. He began with a clear picture of the end in mind and then redesigned to achieve that goal. When asked what he hoped to build at GE, Welch replied, "A decade from now, I would like General Electric to be perceived as a unique, high-spirited, entrepreneurial enterprise...the most profitable, highly diversified company on earth, with world quality leadership in every one of its product lines."[5]

Obviously, all kinds of Design Devils emerged once the goal was identified and clarified. Until that point, GE was getting the exact results it was designed to get. Prior to Jack Welch's time, GE traded at $4 per share. But upon his retirement, this same stock traded at $80 per share. The results changed because the design changed.

Welch wasn't popular in every circle, but everyone knew that popularity was never part of his intended design. He instructed his managers to "fix, sell, or close" uncompetitive businesses. As a result, scores of businesses were sold, including central air-conditioning, housewares, coal mining, and, eventually, even GE's well-known consumer electronics business. Between 1981 and 1990, GE freed up over $11 billion of capital by selling off more than 200 businesses. Within that same time frame, the company made over 370 acquisitions, investing more than $21 billion in such major purchases as Westinghouse's lighting business, Employers Reinsurance, RCA, Kidder Peabody, and Thomson/CGR, a French medical imaging company.

The mandate for a new design changed other factors besides products. It also affected personnel. Besides becoming more "lean and agile," the staff also integrated a high level of discipline. Certain departments received a 50% cut in staff. Remaining employees operated with a unique protocol, asking fellow colleagues, "How do I add value?" or, "How do I make people on the line more effective and competitive?"[6]

Critics blamed Welch for getting rid of the bottom 10% of his employees every year. Yet, that's often the only factoid that many people see. GE worked with all its employees and the ones fired were not surprised when the news came. The result of this particular design alone produced an extraordinarily high-performing organization.

Although Welch utilized many new strategies with his design, his single-focused goal proved successful. *Fortune* magazine ranked GE the nation's most admired company in 1998.[7] This same article provided the reason behind the ranking. "The truth is that no one factor makes a company admirable, but if you were forced to pick the one that makes the most difference, you'd pick leadership."

Warren Buffet agreed with that logic, saying, "People are voting for the artist, not the painting." When the time to count the votes came in, the numbers revealed that Welch had won.

In 1980, the year before Welch became CEO, GE recorded revenues of roughly $26.8 billion. In 2000, the year before he left, revenues were nearly $130 billion. The company went from a market value of $14 billion to more than $410 billion at the time of his retirement, making it the number one most valuable and largest company in the world, up from America's tenth largest by market cap in 1981. In 1999, *Fortune* named Welch the "Manager of the Century," and *Financial Times* recently named him one of the three most admired business leaders in the world today.[8]

In 2006, *Fortune* published another article titled, "What makes GE great?"[9] The subtitle sheds more light: "For the sixth time in the past decade, GE is America's most admired company. Its success does not come easy." The writer attributed the greatness of GE to the design of the company. Although the build and maintain components are necessary to organizations, the devil is truly in the design. Luckily for

GE, Jack destroyed those Design Devils. And those of us who buy GE are better because of it.

Design Devils come in many shapes and sizes, but I've seen five specific ones lurking around more frequently than others. Although I'm continuing with the landscape metaphor, upon further inspection you'll realize these Devils aren't industry specific. Look close enough and you're bound to find them in your world as well.

One word of caution, though: don't try to ignore these Devils. They don't mind if you don't pay them any attention because as long as they exist, they'll sabotage your design no matter how good your intentions. Take courage, nonetheless. Once we understand them, we have the option of eradicating them for good. Here are the infamous five:

Devil 1: Poor Drainage
Devil 2: Context Confusion
Devil 3: High Traffic
Devil 4: Aesthetic Misfit
Devil 5: Short-Sighted Plan

Devil 1: Poor Drainage

We must design who flows in and out of our lives and our organization.

Who we bring on our team is intentional, not accidental. And how we bring them on is by design, not by default. We have a motto within our environment: hire the best and fire the rest. Although simple, it's not simplistic.

Unfortunately, the pattern today is: hire quickly and fire slowly. This ineffective design hurts the entire organization. When mediocrity is tolerated, inefficiency is celebrated. A better design is to hire slowly and fire quickly. This props us up for success and not set-backs.

"Mis-hires" can always happen, but we do everything in our power to avoid them. They're expensive on many fronts. Although numbers differ based on several factors, studies reveal that a mis-hire costs conservatively three times the annual salary of the respective employee. In their book *Topgrading: How Leading Companies Win by Hiring, Coaching, and Keeping the Best People,* Brad and Geoff Smart share their startling research from interviews with more than fifty different companies. The study revealed that for "mid-managers whose base salary is in the $100,000 range, the average cost of mis-hiring is fifteen times base salary, or $1.5 million." Just imagine the pressure for increased profits that's now required just to break even.

Many factors contribute to mis-hires, and unethical choices surrounding the interview process don't help. Incblot, a leading source in organizational psychology, shared that a recent survey found "41% of job applicants admitted to having lied in a job interview" and a 2006 *Forbes* article estimates that 40% of résumés are "not entirely above board.'"[10]

No hire is a guarantee, but we can take measures that drastically improve our odds. We can design who flows in and out and design how this process works.

In landscaping, proper drainage is one of the most overlooked parts of the design. I've seen first-hand how poor drainage can destroy properties. Many times, my company is called in to repair the damage from the poor drainage. Unfortunately, the cost of redesigning is often much more expensive than designing it right the first time.

Poor drainage affects us and our organizations as well. Associating with the wrong people is often much more costly than finding the right people the first time. As a result of this reality, my team has designed certain processes to increase our odds. We've brought in several promising people as interns first and then evaluated how they flow with the rest of our team. We hired my latest assistant for a two-week trial period before we offered her the job.

It goes both ways, though. Proper drainage not only affects the flow that comes in, but also the flow that goes out. Our team spends time designing the way people eventually leave our organization as well as how they initially come into it. We've designed a very intentional exit interview that has helped us dramatically improve areas that we needed to shore up. This additional perspective helps us see the "underground" of our organization. The exit interviews often bring clarity and, in the long run, they've helped us avoid some costly mistakes. Designing proper drainage is an essential part of creating an environment conducive for growth.

Devil 2: Context Confusion

Designing where we place something is just as important as what we place.

In the landscaping world, designing what goes into an environment is often my clients' favorite part. It's fun to pick out fruit trees, water features, and decorative stones. Unfortunately, many of these same clients permit a Design Devil to sneak in unnoticed. Fruit trees are nice, but unless we determine the overall design, we're just inviting clutter and confusion into our space.

Most individuals and organizations suffer from the Context Confusion Devil because we tend to add more and more without proper evaluation. We like the shiniest, the biggest, the newest and the ones with the most buttons and gadgets. If we're not disciplined, we'll keep adding the latest and greatest without focusing on the overall strategy. The result is confusion

For the Starbucks empire, this particular Devil smells like burnt cheese—more specifically, cheddar. I'll explain. Remember 2007? In that year, CEO Howard Schultz wrote an infamous memo complaining about the "commoditization of Starbucks". After gaining major attention through the Internet, these words contributed to the reduction of the company's stock by 42% at year end.

Schultz's frustration stemmed from multiple design flaws, but one smell in particular pushed this Devil to the surface. In his #1 New York Times best-selling book *Onward: How Starbucks Fought for Its Life without Losing Its Soul,* Schultz writes about the burnt cheese Context Confusion Devil that popped up into his awareness. "People who have known me for years will tell you that few things had ever piqued my ire as much as that smell," Schultz writes. "I could not stand it."[11] According to *Fortune* magazine, "having opposed the idea of selling breakfast sandwiches from the get-go, he hated the way 'singed Monterey Jack, mozzarella, and, most offensively, cheddar' from the sandwiches overwhelmed the aroma of coffee."[12] "Where was the magic in burnt cheese?" he wrote, adding, "The breakfast sandwich became my quintessential example of how we were losing our way."

How exactly did Starbucks lose its way? Did they stop making coffee? Did they stop serving muffins and cakes? Did they stop selling travel mugs? Of course not. Instead, they let a few Devils in the backdoor. In an effort to bring more options to their customers, they brought confusion to their context and to their customers. A good thing in the wrong place becomes a bad thing rather quickly.

During 2007, when customers opened the door to a Starbucks, they didn't know if they were in a breakfast shop, a CD store, or a coffee bar. The management didn't know either. Because of context confusion, there was buyer confusion, and this Design Devil sabotaged the profit margin. The only solution was clarity, and that's just what Schultz and his team did.

They changed the design and the results changed too. Less than twenty-four months later, Starbucks reported record earnings for fiscal 2010, with earnings per share up 138% on a 15% gain in revenues. A few months later, they broke their own record again.

Context is king, and we must predetermine our ultimate goal before we start building. If we're causal, we'll just experience casualties. Designing where we place something is just as important as what we place into our environment. On my teams, at every juncture we ask ourselves, "Does the decision we're about to make move us in the direction of our final outcome?" If the answer is yes, we go with it. If not, we avoid it. Little compromises and oversights piled up over time can bring big confusion later. My business partner, Paul Martinelli, says, "I make big things out of little things so that little things don't become big things."

Devil 3: High Traffic

We must design proper pathways to avoid wear and tear in our relationships.

Landscapers cringe when they see a beautifully manicured lawn accented by a well-worn dirt shortcut right through the middle of it. You know what I'm talking about. This Design Devil rears its ugly head in High Traffic spaces. There could be many culprits to blame for this Devil: hedges spaced too far apart, pavers missing from the intended path, or poorly placed flower beds. Regardless of the reason, High Traffic areas demand a high price on the overall environment if we don't design for wear and tear. We can accommodate the tension if we anticipate it, but if unplanned, then we can expect a price tag that demands time and money.

Most organizations also have High Traffic areas that cause wear and tear on relationships. There could be many culprits to blame for this Design Devil: team building events spaced too far apart, performance reviews missing from the culture, or poorly placed employees. Regardless of the reason, High Traffic areas demand a high price on the overall environment if we don't design for the wear and tear. We can accommodate the tension if we anticipate it, but if it unplanned, then we should also expect a price tag that demands time and money.

Just because we have High Traffic areas doesn't mean we're sunk. We can destroy this Design Devil if we're willing to make strategic adjustments. Recently, we had the responsibility of dealing with this Devil on one of our teams. Thankfully, we destroyed it. Here's the story.

Paul Martinelli and I joined John Maxwell and started The John Maxwell Team in March 2011. We designed it well with a certain set of processes and procedures. Unable to anticipate the tremendous High Traffic, we found out rather quickly that something had to give. Luckily for us, we decided it wouldn't be our sanity. Instead, we turned our attention toward designing a proper pathway to avoid wear and tear in our relationships.

Email exchanges with our coaches became a High Traffic area. We were spending time and money trying to equip these quality people with immediate answers. Not an easy job if you factor accommodating a few thousand coaches in nearly 100 countries. In the process, we were burning out our support staff and frustrating the coaches who needed quick answers. Wear and tear defined the environment.

Our new pathway was simple. We created an FAQ page on our website that helped eliminate a good portion of the questions. In addition to the FAQ page, we set up several weekly admin calls where coaches could jump on our conference call system and speak with a real live support person instead of engaging in an email conversation.

The result of this new design was tremendous. We discovered that many coaches struggled with the same issues. Hearing others ask the same question enabled everyone to learn simultaneously and shorten the learning curve. We multi-purposed our call and created a new pathway that cut down on the relational wear and tear. Our support staff now feels more energized and our coaches feel more equipped because we eliminated this High Traffic Design Devil.

Devil 4: Aesthetic Misfit

We must design a good fit: surrounding ourselves with people who believe like we believe, but who think different thoughts.

For some people, a certain wintery month brings a particular Design Devil right along with it. Every December, some of us head out into the wilderness, or at least to a blistery tree farm, with one objective in mind: finding the perfect Christmas tree.

If you've ever watched the Charlie Brown Christmas special on TV, you know that picking the right tree is a very significant task. The other Peanuts characters send Charlie Brown out on a mission to locate the ideal tree. Unfortunately, he gets it all wrong and chooses an unhealthy dilapidated tree.

You know what I'm talking about. Choose a tree too high, too small, too narrow, or too dead and the person who picked that tree could soon be dead. Many times, what looks great at the tree farm looks quite different when brought into our cozy home. That eight foot ceiling really is eight feet tall and that nine foot tall tree still needs a star on top of it.

Translation? Aesthetic Misfit.

Often, we repeat the same mistake when we bring a new person or a new system into our organization. Many times, a candidate looks great at an interview but quite different when brought into our culture. What seemed like a subtle quirk could sabotage our momentum, and that particular department still needs a superstar on top of her game.

Translation? Aesthetic Misfit.

I remember bringing one of these misfits onto my team a few years back. Roger came with raving reviews and a robust résumé. A seasoned purchasing agent from New York, Roger had enough money to comfortably retire from his job and his life. Yet, after four weeks of playing golf, he wanted to re-enter the workforce again and sink his teeth into something with a little more substance than sand traps.

Roger was good at what he did. Motivation, action, and productivity defined his space. Unfortunately, tact didn't. I don't mind someone who thinks differently than me. In fact, I hire with this purpose in mind. But in Roger's case, he also believed differently. He was a misfit, and in no time at all we both realized this reality.

One of my best customers called in on a Friday and asked for some immediate assistance. Roger received the call and insulted my customer and my company with his reply.

"Haven't you heard of a hose?" he caustically shot through the air waves. "Besides," he continued, offending without any hesitation, "you're going to have to wait in line like everybody else. It's Friday and we're slammed."

When I heard Roger's response, I was offended to say the least. No customer should ever be treated with this type of tone. I approached Roger immediately with a clear confrontation in my back pocket. To my surprise, I never even had the chance to deliver my directive. Instead, Roger interrupted me mid-sentence.

"Scottie, you've got a great thing going here. But I am telling you that's the thing that's going to bring you down. You let your customers run the company."

He laid his opinion out with crystal-clear clarity.

"Roger, that's where you and I disagree," I responded firmly. And then after a moment I continued, "You see, I believe the one thing that will help the company move forward is the fact that *we do* listen to the customer."

All my teams embody require unity, not uniformity. We celebrate differences, but we also believe the same things, including our view of our customers. Because our organization clearly designs our beliefs, we can identify the Aesthetic Misfits rather quickly. And in this particular situation, I knew that if Roger didn't go, then our conducive environment would go instead.

Devil 5: Short-Sighted Plan

We must know what we ultimately want, and design with that end in mind.

The Short-Sighted Design Devil kills companies in one of two ways:

1. Because we're short-sighted, we assume something will *stay the same* when, really, *it's designed to change.*
2. Because we're short-sighted, we assume something will *change* when, really, *it's designed to stay the same.*

I'll use a dog and a tree to illustrate the point. First the dog. Then the tree.

Some people buy a little puppy assuming it will stay little. Because their apartment can't accommodate a big dog, if they're short-sighted then they (and their landlord) are in for a big surprise. Many little puppies grow up into massive dogs that need massive space.

Other people buy a little tree assuming it will stay little. Their house looks great with that little tree accenting their small yard. But if they're short-sighted, then they're in for a big surprise when that tree grows to a size of sixty feet.

Comparatively speaking, other people might buy a little puppy assuming it will grow up into a big guard dog and protect their valuables someday. Some dog owners forget that Chihuahuas never make good guard dogs.

Other people buy a little tree assuming it will transform into a massive shade tree and keep the sun away from their front yard. But if these people are short-sighted, then they'll overlook the fact some trees stay little forever. We all know that dwarf trees can't provide shade for an entire yard, much less for that little guard Chihuahua.

The same principle is true for the people in our organization. Sometimes we hire a person based on how we think they'll grow into the job. Realistically though, not all people grow. Some stay small no matter how much we try and "feed" their development.

Other times we hire someone assuming they'll stay the same. They seem like a perfect fit for our open position. Yet, in no time at all, this same person outgrows the job and moves on from our company.

If we don't know what we want and if we don't design with the end in mind, we'll get caught by this Design Devil.

Once we identify the Design Devils and apply the Five Devil Destroyers, we're finally ready to begin building. This is when the real fun happens, when we lace up our boots and step onto the site.

I hope you're not afraid of a few little weeds.

PHASE 2:

BUILD YOUR LEADERSHIP ENVIRONMENT

Step 3:

TEAR OUT, THEN BUILD UP

Prepare the Ground for Your Dream to Take Root

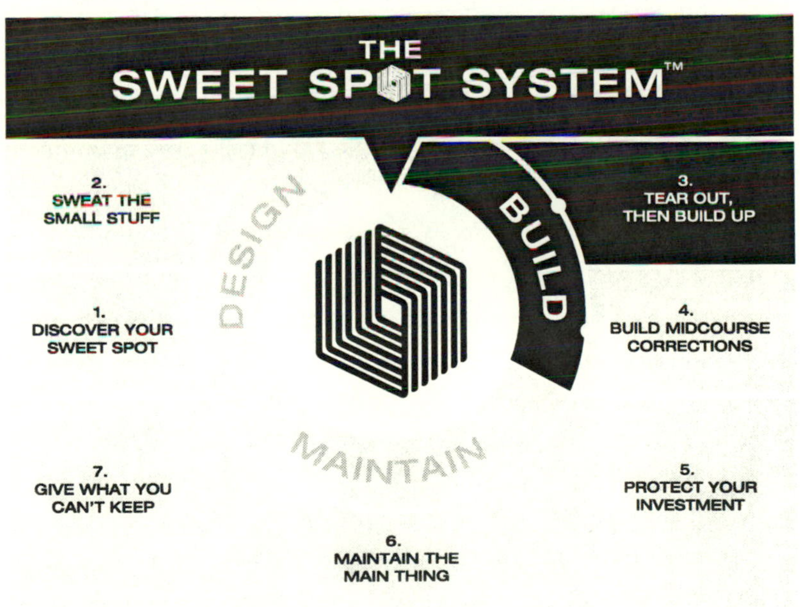

I hate weeds!

Understandably, most people agree with my opinion.

As a professional landscaper, I've never met someone who offered to pay me or my organization to fill his property with weeds. Although disgust for weeds might be universally understood, the definition of a weed isn't. Most people simply don't know the word's true meaning.

Besides the illegal type (i.e., marijuana), weed is "any wild plants growing where it is unwanted and in competition with cultivated plants." According to the official definition, the classification of a weed is based solely upon an environment's design.

Translation?

Weeds are relative.

What might be considered a weed on one person's property might not be on another person's property. Weeds are dependent upon the design of an environment; that is, if there is an intended design.

Unfortunately, some people don't have a design and so, technically, they don't have any weeds either. Although this type of environment might sound good on paper, it's often not pleasing to the eye. The absence of intentional design never wins any awards in landscaping or in life.

Worse yet, if there's no design, then there's no quality control or competition for best ideas or best practices. Without a clear end goal, any strategy proves valid and any initiative plausible. These types of individuals and organizations simply reflect the dialogue between Alice and the Cheshire Cat in Lewis Carroll's *Alice's Adventures in Wonderland.* Confronted with a fork in the road, Alice asked the Cat which road she should take. In a common paraphrase of the dialogue, the Cat replies, "If you don't know where you are going, any road will get you there."[13]

We need a better model than one named Chance or Luck. And thankfully, because of The Sweet Spot System™, we now have one.

In this chapter, we'll explore the third critical step: tear out, then build up. In this step, we prepare the ground for our dreams to take root. Landscapers know most job sites contain weeds, rocks, and other undesirable elements. So, before we can build up, we first need to tear out.

If you've ever pulled literal weeds, you know it's grueling. Not many people enjoy hard work, which is why most individuals and organizations settle on settling.

But I think you'll agree that we need a change. We need more conducive environments because such environments create remarkable products, ideas, and services. So in a real way, we all win when people tear out their weeds. If we avoid this step, we invite average into our environment.

But nature does something else, too. It also reveals the true price of creating an environment conducive to growth. From my experience, I can tell you the required cost isn't cheap.

I know firsthand that if designing, building, and maintaining a physical environment conducive to growth were simple or inexpensive, then everyone would have a meticulously manicured, immaculate lawn. Similarly, if designing, building, and maintaining a leadership environment conducive to growth were simple or inexpensive, then every business would have a carefully crafted, transformational organization.

When I work with my customers in the landscaping business, I often hear them refer to their property as their "dream home." Many of these properties are just that—breathtakingly beautiful. My company is privileged to be the service provider to some of the world's top entertainers, athletes, and celebrities. I say this not to impress you, but to impress upon you the size of investment in some of these dream homes.

No one would think of investing considerable money into their dream home only to let the property around it remain untouched and undeveloped. Quite the contrary. Often my landscaping partner, Tom Balling, reminds us that it's our mission to make the outside space an extension of the inside space. In other words, our customers want our team to make the outside reflect the beauty that's on the inside. The two should match in purpose, design, and value.

Likewise, no one would intentionally think of creating a dream organization, only to let the environment near it remain untouched and undeveloped. We want to see the environment as an extension of the organization. The two should also match in purpose, design, and value.

The first question comes down to our desire.

What do you want?

Admittedly, I don't know all of what you want, but I think I know some. I believe you want to build something significant and worthwhile; something worth writing home about. If not, you wouldn't be reading this book or you wouldn't care about productivity, success, personal development, growth, and legacy. I believe somewhere deep inside you, you long for something more then you've already achieved and attained. It's part of your destiny and part of your dream.

Dreams are interesting, though. I've discovered they're rarely planted in perfect soil. Nature won't allow it. Rather, dreams are forged with effort and intention. Dreams, at least the good ones, always cost more than we estimate and take longer than we initially project.

Prepare yourself. Excuses will always pop up upon the landscape of our dreams. And when they do, we have a choice. We can ignore these weeds and pretend they don't exist. Or, we can take responsibility, roll up our sleeves, and start tearing them out. We can prepare the ground.

People who know me know I don't like excuses. I believe there's only one thing worse than a bad excuse, and that's a good one. We'll always be wooed away with excuses, tempted to trade in our dreams and give up early.

In a deeply personal way, I understand how this can happen. During a dark time in my life, I nearly lost my why and because of it, I nearly lost my way. I let excuses fill up my head and then my heart. I existed unaware, half-dead and half-alive, until one transformational day when I found myself literally on my hands and knees tearing out somebody else's weeds.

But because I changed, everything else changed, too.

Since that day, I've met many other people who gave up on their dreams altogether. Their problem wasn't with their dream, it was with the *design* of their dream and, subsequently, the way they attempted to *build* it. These people never had clarity and so, for them, any weed would do. Like me, they didn't see their excuses as weeds because they didn't know their design. These same people wonder how their lives would have been different if they would have worked, torn out their weeds, and fed their dream. But because they didn't, the only thing they ate was Regret and Remorse.

Not a tasty treat.

Author John Piper warned us about the tendency to give up on desires too easily. He wrote, "Our mistake lies not in the intensity of our desire for happiness, but in the weakness of it."

I am saddened when someone I care about quits on their desires. One of my teammates, Jack—a veteran to the landscaping industry—did just this not too long ago. Subconsciously, he let weeds overrun his dreams.

Jack understood the landscaping trade and worked out in the field. He daily proved his dedication to his job and our entire company.

One small way we observed his commitment took shape at the annual parade in our south Florida town. Each year, our company chooses to be the major sponsor. We toss out 2,500 beach balls to a fired-up crowd. Without exception, Jack was always the first person to show up and the last person to leave the parade. He demanded the job of delivering happiness, all 2,500 expressions of it.

Although he had decades of experience in the landscaping business, he also had a dream for a different role within the company. One hot day he came in from the field and decided to tell me that dream.

"Scott, I'm getting older. Actually, I'm in my fifties now. I have skin cancer, and I need a change. I want to become a salesman."

Jack's dream didn't shock me. In fact, it wasn't even out of bounds. He possessed incredible people skills and I knew, with some training, he could do it. From that point forward, I looked for an opportunity to help him build his dream. Little did I know this chance would come sooner than I thought and, inconveniently, on a day when I was out of town.

Evidently, Jack was in the field doing some work for a customer. Impressed with his skill, the customer asked Jack to quote her a price for redoing the entire property.

Immediately Jack felt overwhelmed. He had never bid a property before and certainly not one at this level. Visibly stressed, he called back to the office and luckily reached Kyle. One of our best salespeople, Kyle told Jack exactly what to do. He conveyed sincere trust and belief.

"Jack, you'll do great. Do the measurements for the property then come back to the office and we'll sketch it out. I'll do the heavy lifting with you and show you the way."

Jack did do the measurements and after some time he returned to the air-conditioned office. Jack produced the measurements and Kyle retrieved a calculator for him. Kyle asked a few clarifying questions. Given the new ground they were covering, Jack seemed out of his element.

Rather than utilizing his optimistic and supportive coach, Jack did something else.

He snapped.

"They don't pay me enough to do this junk," Jack angrily responded, pushing the calculator and papers away in disgust. His self-sabotaging behavior reflected that of a frustrated toddler, not a man in close proximity to his dream. The dialogue continued to go downhill from there.

I returned from my trip only to hear the disappointing report from Kyle. Although Jack eventually ended up getting that bid, his path in getting there was less than favorable. Because I cared about Jack and the company, I knew I couldn't let his negative attitude infect our environment, so I invited him to my office.

"Hi, Jack. Please have a seat," I said, pointing to a chair. I waited until he sat down before I continued.

"Help me understand something? You came into my office recently with an idea. You asked me if you could become a salesman."

"That's right," Jack quickly agreed.

"Whose idea was that?" I inquired.

"Well…mine," he responsibly admitted.

"Jack, you just had an amazing opportunity," I pointed out. "You had the blessing of being mentored by one of the best salespeople I know. Kyle is a veteran in the industry and a superstar in our company. Best of all, he wanted to help you," I explained slowly and methodically. I wanted my words to sink in, hoping Jack realized our cooperative commitment to his success.

"Jack, you recently told me about the hot sun and how it was killing you. I listened and gave you the opportunity to work in an air-conditioned environment," I explained.

By this time, Jack shifted his gaze to the floor, recognizing where this was headed.

"Rather than stepping into this new environment with a desire to grow, you latched onto an excuse. Your statement reveals the environment inside your head right now. And Jack…I'll close with this. I want you to really think about this one."

I paused and then pointedly asked my next question.

"Do your excuses serve your dream?"

The room went quiet.

I think he got the message. Jack realized that to be successful, he would need to tear out his weeds and prepare the ground for his dreams to take root. He couldn't let excuses overrun his environment any longer.

We can't either.

Jack's not the only one who needs to answer this question. We need to ask ourselves, "Do our excuses serve our dream?"

We must answer this question in the build phase. If we get it wrong here, we'll get it wrong in the maintain phase too. I've found three specific actions extremely helpful:

1. **Identify our weeds.** Weeds sometimes hide themselves. Just like Jack couldn't see his weeds initially, we need Truth Tellers to help us be on the look-out.
2. **Own our weeds.** Once we realize an excuse exists, we have a choice. We can either avoid it or we can deal with it. Admitting their existence takes courage.

3. **Eradicate the weeds.** Tearing out our weeds may not be sexy, but it's necessary. Weeds keep growing and stealing our energy until we remove them.

When we pull our weeds, we can't simply cut off the tops. Careless removal just avoids the inevitable. Weeds come back with a vengeance when we don't tear them out by the roots.

I wish I could tell a happy ending about Jack. Unfortunately, he didn't respond to the rebuke. Rather than receiving the truth, he simply avoided it. He proved to be unteachable and eventually I had to remove him from the company. Jack's full story comes later on in our adventure.

Although I hated dismissing him, I knew if I let him remain, his negativity would grow and overrun the entire environment. So, in order for our team to grow, Jack had to go. We had to prepare the ground for our dream to take root.

Who are the Jacks in your world? What's the cost of letting them remain? What's the effect on your environment? What are you sacrificing by letting your weeds continue to grow?

Weeds come in a variety of shapes and sizes; from self-limiting beliefs to self-appointed saviors, from inefficient products to ineffective people. The true question remains: What are you building by letting the weeds remain? The people who matter are the people who are watching. And they're evaluating your leadership by evaluating your response to the weeds.

Before we just start tearing out our weeds, we should first determine if our dream is big enough. Big dreams mean big investments and we need to know if we're going to stay in this spot before we invest more time and money. Logically speaking, why waste time pulling weeds on a plot of ground we're not committed to?

Perhaps an illustration about dream homes and sandcastles might shed a little sunlight on the situation.

I like a certain type of dream. Namely, a big one. I figure if you're going to invest time in doing something, why not make it worth it? I use this approach for everything from work to family time.

On Labor Day a few years back, my family and I visited the beach in Northern Michigan. Every Michigander knows this day in September marks the last official day of summer. After this, the weather is anyone's guess, so we respond by battening down the hatches just in case snow decides to hijack fall.

As a man who loves anything with a motor, I made sure to bring the jet skis. My three wonderful kids—Debby, Andrew, and Jessica—made sure we packed a volleyball, lunch, and some old sand toys. Around 2:00 p.m., I came up with a great idea; at least I thought it was. My kids turned down my idea of building a sand castle. The idea must have been too "small" for them.

Knowing that leadership is influence, I decided to flex my influence muscle by winning over at least one person. I figured because I was someone who teaches on leadership, I should put my lessons into real life. I found someone excited about the concept.[14]

"Hey, Jeffy, I have an idea," I suggested strategically.

"What's that, Uncle Scott?" my young nehew questioned.

Making sure to emphasize certain words, I teed it up with style. "How would *you* like to help *me* build THE WORLD'S LARGEST SAND CASTLE?"

After about two seconds of deep contemplation, Jeffy produced a rich reply, exclaiming, "Yippee!" And with that squeal, we sealed the deal and set out to accomplish our very big dream.

We prepared the ground—a certain section of sand, free from heavy traffic and debris. With a shared design in mind, our strategy took shape by gathering sand, and lots of it. THE WORLD'S LARGEST SAND CASTLE doesn't form itself, so with multiple buckets, we began building a significant pile.

Word began to travel to the other members in our party. Soon, our big dream became infectious and we found more contributors to the cause. Nieces and nephews, uncles and aunts appeared on the scene, engaged and empowered. Bucket after bucket, load after load. Our increasing sand pile stunned even us adults.

But our sandcastle dream quickly morphed into THE WORLD'S LARGEST SHIP, an equally impressive dream. Evidently, the kids felt this was a worthier dream than a simple sandcastle.

The end product proved so. This beauty was outfitted with decks built of sticks and windows built of stones. Debby, Andrew, and Jessica even designed a pool complete with a diving board.

From that experience, I learned that big dreams inspire three things: attraction, memories, and investment.

1. **Big dreams inspire ATTRACTION.** German playwright and poet Johann Wolfgang von Goethe understood this. Besides his spectacular name, he also wrote a spectacular truth related to dreams. He advised us, "Dream no small dreams for they have no power to move the hearts of men." I don't know if Goethe ever designed an impressive ship out of sand, but I do know he designed some fairly impressive works. He dreamed big. And for several centuries, his works have had the power to move our hearts.
2. **Big dreams inspire MEMORIES.** When it came time for our group to take a picture on the beach, we didn't stand by the boat. Rather, we stood *in* the boat! When we talk about that

specific Labor Day, we skip right over the topic of jet skis and volleyball. Rather, we jump into the experience we had and the laughter we enjoyed designing THE WORLD'S LARGEST SHIP. Besides fun, our big dream created a powerful memory.

3. **Big dreams inspire INVESTMENTS.** Although not a popular topic, big dreams come with a price tag; namely, pain. And this isn't a price everyone is willing to pay. We can't simply *show up* and expect to *go up* unless we first choose to *grow up*. We must be mature enough to recognize that a real exchange is required. We must exchange what we have for what we might obtain, and what we have achieved for who we might become.

Big dreams take more effort, but they also make more impact. And my guess is that you want to create big impact.

Creating an environment conducive to growth inside yourself and your organization is a big dream. This is why so few experience it. But just because it's uncommon doesn't mean it's impossible. By examining successful big dreams we observe a universal structure, evident regardless of whether they're related to creating conducive environments. These three phases are: the birth of the dream, the death of the dream, and the rebirth of the dream.

Think about it. Every epic dream died somewhere along the way. People believed the dream was impossible to achieve. Like landing a man on the moon or establishing civil rights or inventing the light bulb or discovering the laws of flight. Refresh yourself with some insightful quotes that reflect the death of a dream:

"It will be years—not in my time—
before a woman will become prime minister."
Margaret Thatcher, future prime minister, October 26, 1969

"Man will not fly for fifty years."
Wilbur Wright, American aviation pioneer, to his brother, Orville, after a disappointing flying experiment in 1901 (their first successful flight was in 1903)

"We are probably nearing the limit of all we can know about astronomy."
Simon Newcomb, Canadian-born American astronomer, 1888

"Rail travel at high speed is not possible because passengers, unable to breathe, would die of asphyxia."
Dr. Dionysys Larder, professor of natural philosophy and astronomy, University College London, 1830

Two out of four of these lethal quotes were uttered by the same people who eventually achieved the same dream they once thought impossible. History reveals a natural cycle.

Big dreams are birthed out of our Sweet Spot—the place where our Purpose, Passion, and Plan intersect. A wise person will plant this seed trusting that it will achieve full maturity. But unbelief, doubt, and skepticism sneak in and spring up like weeds, choking out our belief and best intention.

Observing this opposition, some people surrender their dream. They assume because they can no longer see it that it must be dead and gone forever. Rather than staying with their dream and tearing out their weeds, they move on and try to birth a different dream in a different environment.

They fail to realize that if they stayed with their dream and pulled their weeds, they would have prepared the ground for their dream to take root. For hope to grow, it needs to be cultivated and nurtured.

Weeds of worry and doubt will always spring up quickly, hoping to choke out hope. And bad attitudes only contribute to the cause and feed the weeds.

But for those who stay with their dreams and tear out their weeds, these people witness the rebirth of their dreams. Not all at once, but ever so slowly, like a solitary flower springing up in infertile and unforgiving earth, their dream will poke through above the surface.

It's long and arduous work, but it's also necessary work. Creating a conducive environment means confronting our current one. And changing the overall design requires first changing ourselves.

My dream of owning a large and vibrant landscaping business brought with it a certain set of challenges—weeds, you might say. Initially, I allowed these weeds to spring up. But I stuck with my dream and eventually tore them out one at a time.

You have your own set of weeds trying to kill your dream. These weeds could be doubt, discouragement, self-limiting beliefs, fear, stress, finances, relational damage, or restrictions. How long will you let these weeds flourish?

I'm not minimizing their power. I know they pose a true threat, but I also know you're stronger. Your story isn't one of defeat because you're an overcomer.

Maybe you think these weeds have already killed your dream. Maybe you feel your dreams are beyond repair. If so, don't despair. I've witnessed plenty of rebirths, several of them firsthand.

I understand why people give up on their dreams, I just don't agree with them. Before we create conducive environments in our organizations, we need to create them within ourselves. We can't export hope and belief if our default is discouragement and unbelief. Leaders who believe the world is against them subconsciously export that presupposition into their workplace. We affect those around us.

French-born American author Anaïs Nin wrote, "We don't see things the way they are, we see things the way we are."

When we accept defeat and discouragement, we broadcast that same station to those around is. If unchecked, we play the role of a virus, spreading fear and permitting an environment of victimhood. Blame, accusations, and selfishness spring up like weeds, killing anything good and wholesome.

But the opposite is true, too. We can broadcast another station, creating space for a life-giving environment. This is why it's so important to tear out our weeds and prepare the soil for a rebirth. Obstacles will come. The true test is the perspective we choose when they spring up.

I speak as one who intimately knows "dream death." I've experienced it personally and professionally. I've had my dream clearly within my grasp only to see it killed right in front of me. I've been tempted to give up and give in. But I've also learned that our dreams can outlive death.

Here's what I know. Most people have dreams. Some even embody their dreams. But a select few allow their dreams to outlive them. You know of one such leader. Maybe you've even gone inside and played within his dream. His name was Walt Disney.

Like with any big dreamer, Walt experienced his own dream death. Creators often do. It's a tricky thing to gain support for something that only exists in your mind. But that's where all dreams exist—beneath the surface.

This unseen reality makes some uncomfortable and others confused. We see proof in a powerful example. Soon after the completion of Disney World in Orlando, someone asked Michael Vance, the creative director for Disney, "Isn't it a shame that Walt Disney did not live to see this?" Vance quickly replied, "He did see it, and that's precisely why we are here today."

Life is no respecter of persons. It doesn't play favorites or offer shortcuts. Walt had to decide if he would stick with his dream.

Walt had to tear out his weeds just like everybody else. Walt had to prepare the ground for his dream to experience a rebirth. Walt never stopped building his dream, and for the millions of people who experience Disney World annually, we're sincerely grateful he kept building.

Walt's dream popped through the surface, creating a conducive environment because he understood the principles within The Sweet Spot System™ and not because he simply wished upon a star.

I wish I had known this back in 1988. Unfortunately, I found myself wishing upon a star just to survive. I was a man engulfed in weeds and shockingly, I didn't even know it. Sometimes weeds are like that. They spring up overnight and catch us off guard without us even expecting it.

That summer, I went with my wife back to New York for my sister's wedding. I enjoyed connecting with everyone, but something about my dad puzzled me that day.

Until then, my dad couldn't even spell the word "down." He was always up. At an early age he read Norman Vincent Peale's book *The Power of Positive Thinking*. He loved it so much he gave it to me to read when I was in seventh grade. That book changed him because it gave him tools—like the power of the correct attitude.

My dad believed his attitude set the course of his environment. Because of this, he always chooses to create a positive one—except on that particular day.

That's why he got my attention so quickly.

I found out my dad had just lost his right-hand man within his inner city ministry. Each week, his team bussed 200-300 kids in from a variety of locations in the city. The church even had a small Christian school associated with it. But with his friend's departure, they now they had a huge hole at the school that left the entire ministry vulnerable.

When I heard about my dad's situation, I did what many of us do. I exchanged my dream for his.

Rather quickly, I found a buyer for my business; thus, a buyer for my dream. I sold myself and the landscaping business with that one transaction. When my wife finished student teaching that semester, we moved from sunny Florida to frigid New York where I became the school principal and she a teacher in exchange for a combined weekly income of $120 a week.

The next two weeks were the longest fourteen days of my life. I tried to make it work, but clearly I was out of my Sweet Spot. My work felt contrived and irrelevant, a far cry from where I had just been. Clearly, I wasn't helping anyone. And so I met with my father and relayed my reality to him.

He saw the mismatch, too, and graciously blessed my departure from ineffectiveness. I quickly learned that his right-hand guy changed his mind and was on his way back to serve as principal again. Elated by this news, I felt relief for him and the entire school. Yet here I was, a man with a pocket full of cash and not a purpose in sight.

I had sold my successful landscaping business back in Florida and at the moment I had nothing to show for it. I was a man without a dream and a man without a job. On top of all that, I had a wife and a brand new baby to provide for.

So in that moment, I did what all entrepreneurs do—I got creative and jumped into six jobs over the next three and a half years. I tried everything: roofing, replacing windows, stocking and distributing coin-operated vending and video game machines. I went from a large cash flow to a drop away from bankruptcy.

Eventually, I sold all my toys in order to be mature and practical. In their place, I managed to obtain mononucleosis and a four-month sentence of lying flat on my back. Weeds popped up all over my life and I couldn't see straight enough to know which way was up. A thick dark cloud hung over my awareness. I lacked clarity and, because of it, I lacked confidence, too.

Out of desperation, I made a call back down to Florida and reached out to one of my best vendors, Rood Landscape's companies wholesale nursery. With the tables obviously turned, I had gone from business owner to a man in dire need of a job.

"Hi, Don. This is Scott Fay," I said. Thankfully, he remembered me.

"Look, Don, I am thinking of moving back to South Florida very soon. I wanted to see if you had any openings in your company."

My request contained elements of desperation because I knew this was the only idea I had left.

"Yeah, Scott. We might have something. Tell you what, let's fly you down here so you can meet the team and we can see if it's a fit."

And with that conversation, he booked my flight to Hobe Sound, Florida. Ironically, with that gesture, I heard a sound of hope ringing in my ears—that is, until the owner—Roy Rood, a legend in the industry—delivered the disappointing news to me.

"Well, Scott, it's been an amazing two days with you. You bring something special to the table. And if you're willing to go through the process, the table has something special to bring to you. I want you on our team and so I'm offering you a job–"

Elated, I interrupted. "Mr. Rood, that's great. I'm thrilled!" I couldn't contain my excitement. "This was exactly the hope I'd been looking for."

"...I want to start you at the ground level—literally. So if you want it, you'll be at $8.50 an hour pulling weeds in our nursery."

I couldn't believe the job or the pay he offered. Less than four years prior, I hired Mr. Rood's company to work for me. Now, in a cruel twist, I found myself staring at an offer to come back at literally the lowest position in the company—pulling weeds. As uninviting as the offer appeared, I didn't have any other options.

Immediately, I moved my family back to South Florida.

The contrast killed me. I had left landscaping three and a half years before with dignity. I now returned with humility. I had departed with a brand new red and cream Bronco 2. I returned with a Buick Skylark held together with duct tape and Velcro. I left having just sold a fleet of trucks. I returned craving the opportunity to own just one truck. I left a beautiful house and I returned to a duplex in a low-income part of town. We left with a solid group of friends who we visited on the weekends, but we returned with a baby daughter and the inability to afford take-out pizza.

Then it happened—my breaking point.

A typical August day defined with atypical heat, I found myself down on my hands and knees soaked in sweat. I looked beside me and saw day laborers performing the same task as me—pulling weeds. Here I was, a former business owner who went to college, and now I was working for an hourly wage doing an entry level job. I knew many of my co-workers had never even attended high school and I wondered how I fell so far so fast.

Beads of sweat now mixed with tears rolled down my cheeks. I wiped off my face and looked up to the heavens. I felt abandoned and alone. Little did I know the transformation that would evolve from my perspiration.

By pulling Mr. Rood's weeds I was actually pulling my own too. God knew I needed to prepare the ground for my own dreams to take root. That day, I had no idea I'd purchase Mr. Rood's business someday and become the CEO of one of the leading landscaping companies in the country. Little did I know, just how much "the table" would bring to me.

The weeds I tore out that day were pride and arrogance; two weeds that kill many individuals and organizations. I couldn't build up without first going down to the bottom, all the way down to my hands and knees.

Today, I'm not done pulling my weeds.

Don't get me wrong. In some ways, it would be comforting to think I was done with weed-pulling. But in a sense, it would be a chilling thought as well.

I've realized that as long as I'm dreaming, I'll always be pulling my weeds. Dreams bring death with them. It's just part of the cycle. With the birth of a dream comes the death of a dream and, for the select few who are willing to stick with it, the rebirth of a dream. Nature has a funny way of incorporating this into the system. I've seen it in landscaping and I've seen it in life.

Initially, death may look like our biggest threat, but in reality it's not. There are many things more frightful then death, like an unlived life for example. As Anaïs Nin accurately pointed out, "People living deeply have no fear of death."

Physical death simply reveals the legacy we've left. This is the benefit of designing, building, and maintaining an environment conducive to growth.

Upon deeper reflection, maybe I'll change my mind. Maybe I don't hate *every* type of weed. Maybe just the literal ones. I guess the metaphorical ones make us sharper and stronger.

Still, if we're going build up, we must first tear out. We must prepare the ground for our dream to take root.

Step 4:

BUILD MIDCOURSE CORRECTIONS

Blessed are the Flexible for They Shall Not Break

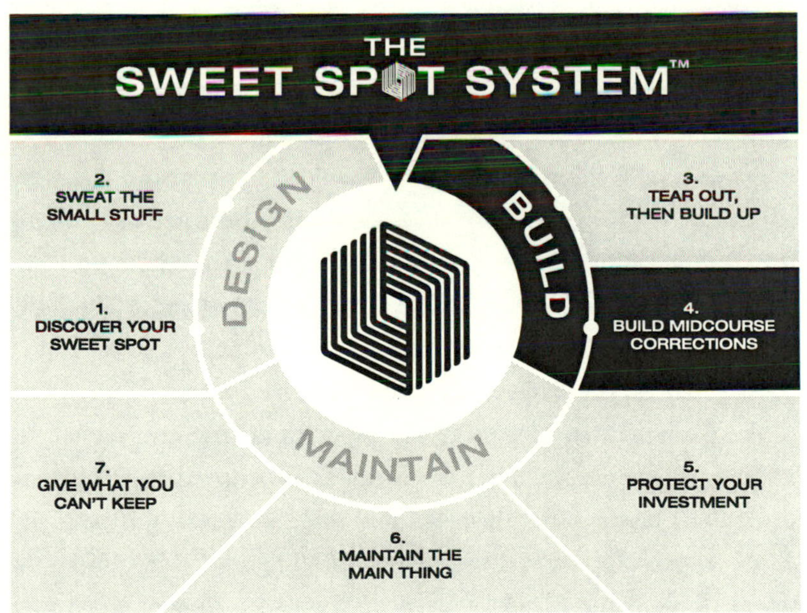

In life, plans are a great idea. In landscaping, they're even more than that—they're essential. Working without any plans proves unwise and ineffective.

But in spite of the significance of plans, I've also learned to hold them loosely. Our team understands the importance of flexibility because inflexible plans only end up breaking two things: people and relationships.

Any navigator will tell you about the critical need for midcourse corrections. According to Dictionary.com, a midcourse correction is a "navigational correction made during the course of a ship, airplane, rocket, or space vehicle at some point between the beginning and end of the journey."[15]

Pilots in particular understand the reality of fluidity—that nothing ever goes perfectly according to plan. Regardless of the amount of preparation and training, unforeseen variables will always arise, like ever-changing weather conditions and even uncommon bird strikes.

Chances are you're very familiar with one of the most famous midcourse corrections of all time. Thanks to the pilot's successful adjustments, the passengers were spared and the true story is now retold often.[16] But a deeper look reveals the story behind the story.

The flight from LaGuardia Airport in New York City to Charlotte/Douglas International Airport began rather routinely. A group of 155 people boarded the plane on that chilly January afternoon, only aware of the plans written in their datebook or smart phone. Neither the 150 passengers nor the five crew members anticipated the midcourse corrections that awaited them roughly three minutes into the flight. As the aircraft approached the George Washington Bridge during the initial climb, it hit a flock of Canada Geese with six-foot wingspans, weighing eight to eighteen pounds each. The pilot later explained that the Canada Geese sounded like large hail pelting the plane.[17]

Immediately, the aircraft lost thrust in both its engines.

A bleak situation instantly turned even bleaker. An aircraft topped off with full fuel tanks descended quickly upon a densely populated Manhattan. This former airliner—now turned bomb—dropped from the sky, speeding toward a mass of humanity.

The fate of those *in* the plane and the fate of those *below* the plane were now intimately tied to the action or inaction of the responsible pilot 57-year-old Captain Chesley B. "Sully" Sullenberger. This former fighter pilot had been a commercial airline pilot since leaving the United States Air Force in 1980. Luckily for the people involved, Captain Sully was also a safety expert and a glider pilot. The "glider" part enabled the exact midcourse correction needed during the exact moment following the unexpected bird strike.

Air traffic control personnel tried their best to provide a solution, shouting out alternative locations to land, but their suggestions only served as a distraction. They had no idea how desperate the situation actually was. Although losing two engines was not part of Sully's original plan, he remained flexible and made the necessary adjustments *on the fly,* even though his plane couldn't fly.

He eventually ditched the airliner near the USS *Intrepid* museum. Upon landing in the Hudson River, the airliner sank slowly, but nearby ferries and boats ensured a complete and safe evacuation. Not one person perished, thanks to Sully's critical midcourse correction.

The industry acknowledged Sully's appropriate actions, describing it as "the most successful ditching in aviation history." The entire crew of Flight 1549 received the Master's Medal of the Guild of Air Pilots and Air Navigators. The award citation read, "This emergency ditching and evacuation, with the loss of no lives, is a heroic and unique aviation achievement."

But not everyone agreed.

Many dismissed January 15, 2009, as a fluke or an example of luck in its purest form. The bulk of society preferred to label the whole experience as a miracle. They called it the "Miracle on the Hudson."[18]

But a closer examination proved it wasn't a miracle.

Captain Sully told CBS news anchor Katie Couric in an interview, "My focus at that point was so intensely on the landing. I thought of nothing else." Although the midcourse correction was completely outside his plan for that day, he never doubted his decision. "It just took some concentration. I was sure I could do it."

Students of leadership understand the fine line between confidence and arrogance. Sully had a deep humility for the situation at hand, but also a strong resolve that he could do something about it. He was prepared for the moment and so the moment was prepared for him.

He told Couric, "For 42 years, I've been making small, regular deposits in this bank of experience: education and training. And on January 15 the balance was sufficient so that I could make a very large withdrawal."[19]

Sully's large withdrawal paid great dividends for everyone involved and everyone would agree that humanity is much richer because of him.

Within Sully's situation, we observe a unique set of principles relative to Step 4: Build Midcourse Corrections. I call these **The Four Core Corrections**. Let's identify and unpack them.

1. **Intersect the issue.** Sully knew what happened when the aircraft hit the birds. Technically, he could have distanced himself from the issue at hand, but instead he intersected it.

For the first time that day, the captain took control of the plane. "My aircraft," Sully said. "Your aircraft," said the first officer.[20] And with those two words, Sully took responsibility for the situation.

2. **Correct the problem.** Sully didn't take a poll. He didn't even let air traffic control shape his split second thinking. Time was of the essence and only he understood the severity of the situation. Rather than trying to reroute to another airport, he knew his decreasing altitude demanded an immediate midcourse correction.
3. **Protect the goal.** Captain Sully never lost sight of the goal. In times of crisis, many people change the goal instead of changing the plan. Thankfully, Sully didn't. Instead, he changed the plan and protected the goal by landing safely and saving everyone on board.
4. **Reflect the outcome.** Captain Sully reflected the intended outcome to his co-pilot and crew. He embodied a perfect landing because he knew he could do it. He depicted a calm but strong resolve, never projecting fear or incompetence. And upon landing safely, like all good leaders, he reflected upon the outcome.

The Four Core Corrections can be applied within landscaping as well as life. Many times, my teams and I utilize these four principles when interfacing with our landscaping clients. Just like Sully's experience, we always start with a plan, but every landscaper knows the truth—the site appears much different from the plans. There will always be unanticipated rocks, unseen obstacles, and uneven grading.

When we step foot upon a site that proves different from the original plan, here's how we proceed:

1. **Intersect the issue.** When there's a gap between expectations and experience, we have a couple choices. We can either ignore the issues or we can intersect the issues. I prefer the latter. The former puts us in a defensive posture. The latter puts us in an offensive one. We can only help our clients when we get involved.
2. **Correct the problem.** With action comes opportunity. Movement allows us the option of correcting the problem. By utilizing this principle, we can work with our clients and offer them solutions.
3. **Protect the goal.** We never take our clients for granted. Their satisfaction is our highest goal and our team always protects this. Even though our plan sometimes changes, our goal remains constant.
4. **Reflect the outcome.** In landscaping, nothing ever goes perfectly according to plan either. Orders change. Deliveries show up late. Products get put on back order. Yet, with all these adjustments, we must continually reflect the intended outcome—a job well done. We can't project fear or incompetence. Instead, we must depict a calm and strong resolve. And like all good teams, we must always reflect upon the outcome.

What about you?
What about your context?

What's your response when you experience a situation that deviates from the predetermined plan?

Do you get angry?

Do you become fearful?

Do project a calm and strong resolve?

Do you plan for adjustments to the plan?

Do you build in midcourse corrections?

Do you practice The Four Core Corrections?

Do you intersect the issue?

Do you correct the problem?

Do you protect the goal?

Do you reflect the outcome?

Although intellectually I know The Four Core Corrections, I don't always use them. Like anyone else, I sometimes need to be reminded of them. Recently, I forgot to build midcourse corrections. I discovered that I didn't plan for adjustments to the plan. This particular situation wasn't on a site, but rather on a stage. Maybe that was the problem. Regardless, my business partner, Paul Martinelli, helped me save the day. And this particular day was in desperate need of saving.

"You can't be serious," replied one of my team members. "Yeah, can't you do something about it?" asked another one, politely, yet pointedly.

None of us believed the news our host just casually shared with us. But to his surprise, we didn't find anything casual about it.

"I'm afraid not." Our guide wasn't about to budge.

And with that pronouncement, we now had a choice. In less than twenty-four hours, the room where we currently stood would be filled with 750 attendees from all over the world. During the last few months, our team had invested careful attention to create the perfect environment for this particular day.

We had planned for every possible detail—that is, except the curve ball that had just come speeding into our awareness. We had the convention center guide to thank. Evidently, he thought the day before the big event was the perfect time to inform us about the noisy neighbors we'd soon encounter.

According to his report, 1,000 teenagers were scheduled to fill the adjacent room for their annual youth conference. No worries yet, except that they also booked a rock band complete with extra doses of decibels and bass.

On a normal day, this might have been tolerable, perhaps even acceptable, but this would be no ordinary day. Our team had booked our own major event—three keynote speakers for a full-day seminar. Framed as an educational experience, the event invited 750 attendees to invest in their future by purchasing a ticket to help them develop their craft. They would be arriving with the clear expectation of receiving expertise from three world-class gurus.

The convention center personnel should have known better. We had the contract, that outlined our terms, and we could have probably fought them if we chose to do so. But given the situation, we chose to control something else that day—our attitudes.

Paul Martinelli, the one responsible for setting up the seminar—wisely helped me and the rest of the team recalibrate our outlook. According to the preset agenda, I had the responsibility of starting the seminar and setting the tone for the entire day.

Given the circumstances, utilizing Paul's keen insight, we immediately put our heads together and built a midcourse adjustment. I knew that serving as the emcee, whatever frequency I chose to broadcast would be picked up by the attendees and obviously influence the environment. Rather than react to the annoying interruption at some point in the day, I chose to intersect the issue and address the disturbance before it happened. Although I couldn't control the environment, I could control myself. And I knew if I did that effectively, I'd have a chance of influencing the larger environment. So, I picked up the microphone and addressed the audience.

"Hello, folks. My name is Scott Fay and, like you, I'm thrilled to be here. We have an amazing day planned for you with content from some of the best experts in the industry. You'll have the opportunity to learn and grow and ask questions. We might even have some fun along the way. Our team is here to help you and we're committed to your personal success.

"As a brief aside, I want to make a quick comment. I'd like to give a relevant quote from my favorite book. It says, 'Today I am giving you the choice between a blessing and a curse.'

"At some point in the day, we might hear some noise coming from the room next door. When you hear that sound, you have a choice to interpret it as a blessing or a curse. You see, on the other side of these walls, 1,000 teenagers have gathered to worship their Creator. These same teens could be out doing drugs, bullying, or joining gangs. Instead, they're assembling to offer praise to their God. How you choose to interpret that noise is completely up to you, and it will affect the way you receive the content today."

At that point, I paused momentarily to catch my breath. Although I intended to start again with some general announcements, to my surprise, I couldn't.

The room spontaneously erupted during my split-second respite. All 750 attendees applauded and cheered for the inevitable distraction that awaited their immediate future. They predetermined their response by perceiving the upcoming bass as a blessing and not a curse. Their choice dramatically affected the way we all learned that day. And, best yet, not one person complained about the noise that came pouring into our room during the afternoon session. Our collective internal environment overtook the loud external one at the convention center that afternoon. Together, we created an environment conducive to personal growth.

My goal was clear that day: to set the tone of the entire seminar. Our team had a plan to achieve that goal, but outside of our control, that plan changed. As emcee, I needed to correct the problem by first correcting my outlook. My obvious midcourse adjustment was my attitude. In the words of the late Zig Ziglar, after I did my "check-up from the neck up," I knew I had subtly allowed my circumstances to shape my attitude. Luckily, I caught it before I broadcast it to others.

That morning, I practiced The Four Core Corrections. I intersected the issue by adjusting the plan. I then corrected the problem by correcting my attitude. The audience responded to my challenge and, because of their choice, we collectively protected the goal. And to top it off, we reflected the outcome we wanted—getting better at our craft.

That day, we all made a clear commitment. We decided we wouldn't let a little noise stop us from learning and growing. If we failed to be flexible, I'm convinced that some of us would have broke. Instead, we built a few midcourse corrections.

Personally, I'm thrilled we only encountered a bass strike and not a bird strike. I'll save those other ones for Captain Sully.

Phase 3:

MAINTAIN YOUR LEADERSHIP ENVIRONMENT

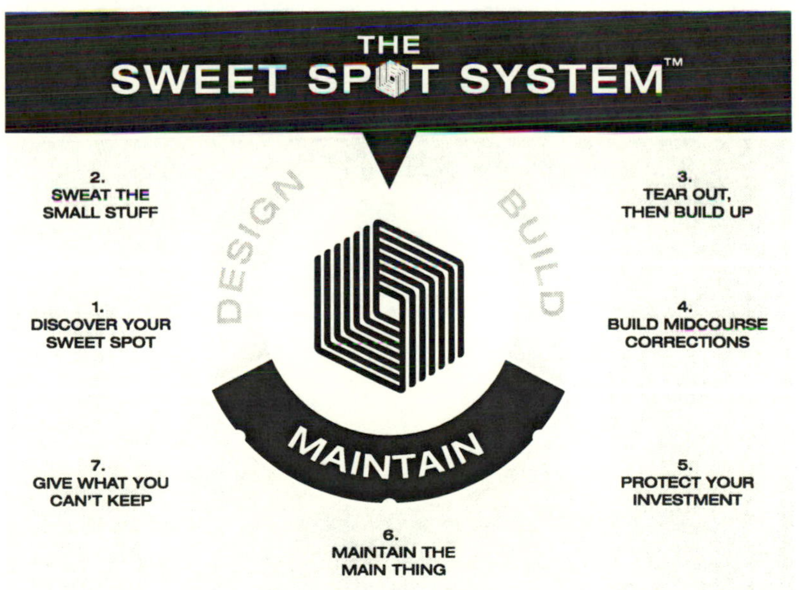

Step 5:

PROTECT YOUR INVESTMENT

Poor Maintenance Costs You More in the Long Run

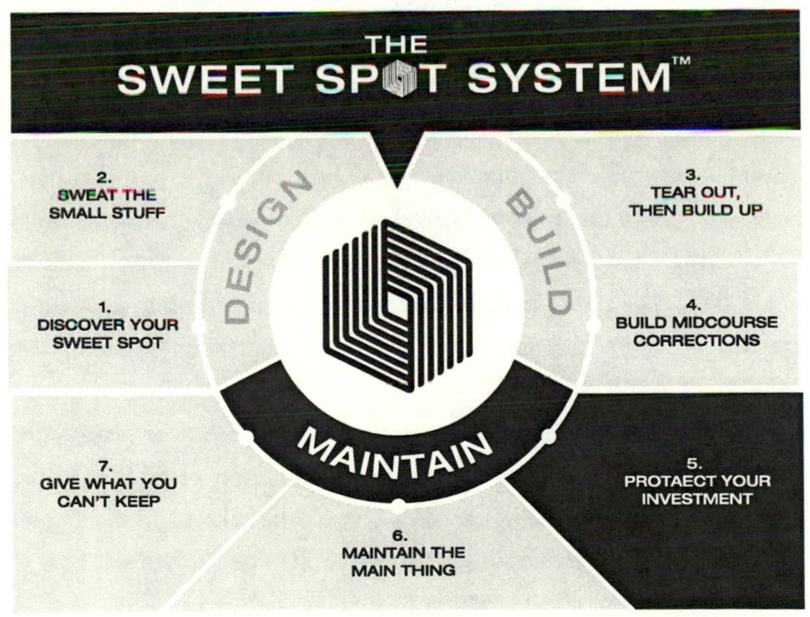

Every four years, the world shows up.

Of course, the city is chosen well before they come. The flights are booked and the hotel reservations fill up.

Every four years.

The building sites for the athletic facilities are chosen. The supplies are flown in and the stadiums fill up for those precious few days.

Every four years.

The athletes are chosen, all according to their time trials. The families fly in and the stomachs fill up on food native to the lucky location.

But is the location of the summer Olympics truly lucky?

Athens spent 15 billion. Four years later, China spent 40 billon. London's final numbers won't come in for a couple more years. Each country seems to outdo the country before. But we've started to see a trend. Except that some experts now categorize this trend as a curse.

In her article "Architectural White Elephants: Beijing, London, and the Post-Olympics Curse", Melinda Liu exposed the undesirable reality. She wrote, "Once the razzle-dazzle of the Summer Games' closing ceremonies fades, one question always pierces the post-Olympics hangover: can all that construction avoid being called a white elephant?"[21]

Beijing's famous "Birds Nest" has been almost completely unused since the 2008 games ended. There was talk of building a mall and hotel next to the stadium, but they have been talking about that for more than four years now.

Some local professional teams attempt to use the abandoned stadiums; however, no team wants to play in front of 50,000 empty seats. Some of the structures are so big that when the Olympic crowds are gone, the local teams simply don't have a large enough fan base to justify maintaining the arenas.

The Associated Press shared its commentary regarding the curse, too. Writer Elena Becatoros humorously pointed out the only ones still using the training pool in Athens are frogs. "They appear to delight in sitting on debris that floats on the half-filled pool's murky waters."[22]

Not everyone in Greece thinks it's funny.

The abandoned Olympic venues are "the focus of great public anger as the country struggles through a fifth year of recession and nearly three years of a debt crisis that has seen a surge in poverty and unemployment."[23]

Host countries invest a large amount of time and money *designing* the athletic structures. They invest even more in *building* them. However, once the games end, the host countries are often unable to *maintain* these multimillion dollar mammoths.

The cost requires a steady cash flow. True, the price of maintenance is small compared to the design and build phase. But in spite of the cost, most host countries have little strategy or funding beyond the games. Every host wants to stand tall on the world stage, so they pour everything into those two weeks with very little to show post-Olympics.

The Hellenic Olympic Committee's president, Spyros Kapralos, admits there was no post-Olympics development plan in 2004. "In their rush to get venues completed, Olympic planners overlooked other crucial factors such as environmental strategy and forward thinking. They also failed to draw up economic feasibility studies or even a basic business plan. Very few of the facilities have been successfully exploited commercially."[24]

Because Greece can't afford the upkeep for its facilities, its own Olympians now train in Cyprus. "We can't use them or even maintain them," says the national coach. "They're just standing there falling to pieces. It's absolutely scandalous. It's as if the lights went out at the closing ceremony and that was it."[25]

The public has seen and felt the scandal.

The Guardian writer Helena Smith shares more details about the public's disapproval. "Athens's Olympic park, once billed as one of the most complete European athletics complexes, is no testimony to past glories. Instead, it is indicative of misplaced extravagance, desolation, and despair."[26]

Smith quotes a local resident. "They've let the whole place go to pot," says Dimitris Dimitriou, a bank worker. "The main stadium is a bit better off because it's used by football teams but, if you look around, everything is rotting and rusting. The toilets are filthy, the showers stink and there's no hot water. I don't think anything here has been cleaned for years."[27]

Every four years?

We could only hope. But unfortunately, we see this pattern more frequently. Much more. This reality plays out daily all across our world on a smaller scale. Maintenance often falls by the wayside. But if you want to save yourself a bunch of pain, remember that although good maintenance costs, poor maintenance costs even more.

Many people believe they can cut corners on maintenance or avoid it altogether. However, letting nature take its course never ends up in a pretty place. We have to wonder, why invest considerable money in the design and build phase without factoring in the maintain phase?

Most people, except for those who sit on Olympic committees, see the wisdom in maintaining physical assets like stadiums and sports arenas. However, the bulk of businesses and organizations don't have these types of assets. Rather, they identify people as their greatest asset, not properties.

But if people are truly our greatest asset, then how do we maintain those assets? And can those assets be improved and developed? Or just like the post-Olympic curse, do organizations need to suffer from a post-hire curse too?

A deeper dig reveals how Step 5: Protect Your Investment, relates to people just as much as stadiums.

Organizations could improve drastically by first improving their people. Unfortunately, most organizations only pay attention to two of the three required components below and therefore, they fall far short. Here's how we protect our people utilizing the **3 Phases of The Sweet Spot System™**.

- **Investment One: Design your team.** Organizations typically spend a considerable amount of time designing job descriptions. A job description serves several purposes including "job identification (title, designation, location) and a statement of duties and functions of a prospective or existing employee."[28] Once the job description is finished, then it's time to build the team.
- **Investment Two: Build your team.** We all try making our hires strategic ones that will advance our mission, vision, and core values. The best organizations outperform their competitors utilizing the intangibles (culture, people, synergy). The tangibles (technology, office supplies, software) rarely give companies an edge over their competition. Remember, the wrong team can turn your dream into a nightmare.
- **Investment Three: Maintain your team.** Of the three phases, this one is the most overlooked. Similar to designing and building an impressive Olympic arena, many organizations design and build an impressive team. They post their job descriptions on the trendiest internet sites. They integrate the hottest personality tests and profiles. They implement a rigorous interview process and pursue the best résumés. But then they stop. Just like the Olympic host countries and their stadiums, these organizations expect their people to develop on their own. But most don't.

It's worth asking. Why improve your people? There are many reasons. For starters, we should invest in our people because we value them. People usually only invest time and money in things that hold value in their hearts.

Gallup put hard data around this seemingly "softer" side of leadership in the workplace. The organization studied more than one million employees across hundreds of organizations and identified the twelve key dimensions that exist in the most productive work groups.[29]

1. I know what is expected of me.
2. I have the materials and equipment to do a job right.
3. I have the opportunity to do what I do best every day.
4. In the last week, I have received recognition or praise.
5. Someone at work seems to care about me.
6. Someone at work encourages my development.
7. My opinions seem to count.
8. I am connected with the mission of my organization.
9. My coworkers are committed to doing quality work.
10. I have a best friend at work.
11. In the last six months, someone has talked to me about my progress.
12. In the last year, I have had opportunities at work to learn and grow.

Notice how many of these dimensions are tied to the employees' perception of the value the organization places on them. I counted that at least ten of the twelve dimensions are directly tied to effective employee maintenance. Breaking them down will help us understand the logic behind the list.

1. I know what is expected of me.

Whenever we hire people, we make sure they understand the expectations beyond their job description. Great teammates don't simply follow the letter of the law and perform up to the job, they go beyond it. For example, there is nothing in our job descriptions that tell our team when they can take off for vacation. However, our organization would suffer if everyone in a certain department took off at the same time. Unwritten expectations that are clearly communicated help us protect the healthy culture that sustains our company.

2. I have the materials and equipment to do a job right.

I'm a firm believer of getting people the right tools to do the best job possible. We can't help our team excel if we're not sure what tools they need. As a result, we build in communication pathways so our people can express what type of equipment they need to get the job done effectively. Nothing murders momentum more than good-natured people feeling ill-equipped.

3. I have the opportunity to do what I do best every day.

We strive to get the right people doing the right things. Author Jim Collins standardized a powerful metaphor in his bestseller *Good to Great*. He presented a compelling rationale for getting the right people on the right seat in the bus. In our organization, we've had the right person in the wrong position a time or two. The wrong position is one that doesn't allow our people to do what they do best every day. This not only sabotages individuals, but also the entire organization. Teammates feel most alive when they're empowered to offer their biggest contribution on a daily basis.

4. In the last week, I have received recognition or praise.

Although we might hide it well, we each have an internal engine and that engine can lose power over time. The ancients believed our internal engine was our heart. Ironically, the junk of life has a unique tendency of damaging our heart. We use phrases to describe this tendency: lost heart, broken heart, half a heart, etc. Although we lose heart, we can get it back through encouragement. To encourage literally means to give heart. An ancient king said, "The right word sustains the weary."[30] Giving people weekly recognition and praise is one of the easiest and most powerful ways to protect your biggest asset—your people.

5. Someone at work seems to care about me.

When people feel like they don't matter, they typically act out negatively in one of two ways. They either underperform or anti-perform.[31] The first tendency is tougher to catch. People who underperform simply live up to the standards others place upon them. Since no one seems to notice them, they don't do much.

The other tendency is just as toxic, but much more noticeable. When people feel like no one cares, they get others' attention by anti-performing. Their rebellious response sticks out and gets them the attention they crave, albeit negative attention.

6. Someone at work encourages my development.

We usually only invest time and money on people and things that matter. When teammates see we're willing to invest in them, most often they reciprocate by investing more deeply into the organization. People display commitment and loyalty toward an organization that makes a commitment toward their long-term development.

7. My opinions seem to count.

If people feel like their opinions count, they share them. If they share them, they feel ownership. If they feel ownership, they are committed. If we don't care what our people think, we'd better be prepared to get new people.

8. I am connected with the mission of my organization.

One of our core needs is significance. Look at charities. They exist on the basis of purpose, not profit. Their volunteers give of their time, talents, and treasures because they believe in the cause behind the charity. Similarly, if we want our teammates to thrive within our organization, we must make our mission clear and provide our people specific ways to connect with that mission.

9. My coworkers are committed to doing quality work.

We all want to be part of a winning team where people love each other *and* the work they do. Nothing kills culture faster than an organization that rewards poor performance. Sometimes, rewards are simply managers who look the other way and tolerate mediocrity. A few bad apples, left to thrive, can kill good morale and poison a healthy culture.

10.I have a best friend at work.

When people experience real community, they're more inclined toward engagement in the workplace. Real relationships help teammates humanize their work experience. We can't expect our people to invest dozens of hours every week if they feel disconnected from people during that time. Real relationships create a shared experience and make the workplace richer.

11. In the last six months, someone has talked to me about my progress.

Pay alone simply isn't enough. People are created with a desire for a fuller expansion and a fuller expression. If six months have passed and no one notices a teammate's progress, that individual isn't likely to continue growing. Although everyone measures appreciation differently (paid vacation days, promotions, recognition), everyone enjoys it when their efforts are noticed.

12. In the last year, I have had opportunities at work to learn and grow.

Engaged people don't like feeling stuck. They want to grow and excel. If organizations don't provide their teams with opportunities to thrive, then they'll find opportunities elsewhere, usually in other organizations. It's been said that people don't quit a company, they quit a person. Intelligent managers provide their people with clear steps to improve and maintain personal growth.

Besides making our people feel valued, there are other reasons that should incentivize our need for employee maintenance, some even related to productivity and profitability. Research reveals a direct correlation between the success of a company and the amount of money invested in growing their people.

Forbes contributor Josh Bersin—director of the leading provider of research-based membership programs in human resources, talent, and learning—provided additional insight in his article "It's Not the CEO, It's the Leadership Strategy that Matters".[32] He wrote, "The companies that rank top in leadership development maturity invest 30-40% more money in leadership than their peers and spend almost 35% more per manager on development than others."

Although it is somewhat common sense, if a company wants to *do* better it must *be* better. Developing people is the most direct strategy to accomplish this goal.

Patricia O'Connell, management editor for *Businessweek.com*, revealed how great companies develop great leaders. According to her research, GE and Zappos—both named among the 20 Best Companies for Leadership in a *BusinessWeek.com*/Hay Group survey—put a premium on selecting, developing, and retaining strong leaders at every level.

She wrote, "What sets them and the other companies on the list apart, however, is not just their emphasis on good leadership, but also how they approach it. They carefully tailor their developing leaders to fit their unique business strategies and organizational cultures."[33]

In other words, both of these companies don't stop at designing and building great teams. Rather, they also maintain great teams by continuing to invest in their people post-hiring.

You're probably wondering how much money we're talking about. How much do companies need to spend to effectively maintain the growth of their employees?

You might think it would cost a small fortune, but the amount might surprise you. Similar to the Olympic example, the cost of maintaining is small compared to designing and building. According to Bersin, "Top companies spend $3,500 and up per manager (more than twice this at senior levels)."

Therefore, the annual investment in maintaining the growth of our people is often less than 5% of their annual salary and benefits package.

Not a whole bunch, but sadly most organizations look at that 5% as an unnecessary expense rather than a critical investment. Shortsighted planning, similar to that of Olympic host countries, bankrupts businesses all across the world. Just as we witnessed impressive Olympic structures deteriorating because of a lack of physical maintenance, so many organizations witness their impressive hires deteriorate because of a lack of professional maintenance.

In tough economic times, usually leadership development for employees is the first thing to go. However, the best companies recognize that this type of rationale is backwards. Why would anyone eliminate investing in their greatest asset when times are tough?

The most critical time to invest is when every other organization isn't. John Larrere, director of the Hay Group agrees. His research reveals that the best companies at "developing leaders recognize the value of strong leadership in both the good times and the bad. Culturally they just cannot do away with leadership development, even in a recession. They don't see it as a perk but as a necessity."[34]

This type of forward thinking is characteristic of those organizations that embody The Sweet Spot System™. In one of the toughest economic times for the landscaping industry, when many others are folding and going bankrupt, our company is posting record numbers.

Do we have better technology or equipment? Not really. The number one thing that's helping us advance is our people. We've designed, built, and maintained an environment conducive to improving and developing our people.

One of the ways we protect our investment is through our Monday morning 7:58 a.m. team meetings. Of course, these meetings contain some updates and briefing, but all through the lens of leadership. When a concern is brought up, immediately a solution is identified and a strategy implemented. Because we've practiced hard as a team, we're able to cut through much of the verbal static and get straight to the point.

We choose mutually understood word pictures with meaning behind them. One of our favorite word pictures is a beach ball which helps us maintain an effective culture. We borrow this imagery from the book *Fierce Conversations* by Susan Scott.[35] She explains how, within organizations, we can get locked into our own perspective. All we see is our side of the beach ball, whether white, blue, green, yellow, or red. Because it's all we see, we don't think any other colors exist. We fail to realize other departments have their own vantage point and their own perspective because they see a completely different color.

If we only make decisions from our perspective, we'll miss the richness of other angles. Myopic organizations usually don't perform well in the long run. And if we want to stay sharp, we need to see the entire beach ball and thereby all perspectives.

Our beach ball word picture helps protect our investments in other ways, too. Oftentimes in our Monday morning meetings, we'll preface a potentially charged conversation by starting it with a phrase like, "From my side of the beach ball…." When a teammate uses this verbiage, we all know that what's coming next is an opinion and not an attack. This type of high emotional intelligence helps everyone play smarter. We have a high level of trust and a low tolerance for innuendoes. Our track record is long and our grievances are short.

In every Monday morning meeting, we know what's expected. If we show up on time, we know we're late. If we show up early, we know we're in for a few leadership nuggets served up fresh. We're not perfect and we're not afraid to tell each other because we're fooling ourselves if we think they don't already know.

Our health is evident. Our culture is contagious. And our care for one another is not only felt, but also expressed. I know most organizations conduct weekly team meetings, too. Although I'm not sure of everything that occurs in these gatherings, I've heard some horror stories. I've heard about pretense and silos, about corporate Kool-Aid and gossip groups. Colleagues in other organizations regretfully loathe their ineffective structures, their internal politics, and their inefficient red tape. Most of these meetings are defined by sideways energy instead of forward motion. Our organization dares to be different.

We've designed, built, and maintained an environment that's intentionally unorthodox. I've always appreciated the observation by J.D. Houston: "If you want something you've never had, you must be willing to do something you've never done."

This quote can be simply hung on a wall or it can be lived out in real time with real teams and real customers. We've chosen to believe that it's possible. We've had to break many traditional beliefs in order to get here. But we believe it's worth it.

Like our view of promotions.

Some people are surprised when they find out that we don't promote people. We don't even believe in it. Instead, we create an environment where people promote themselves. I learned a long time ago that I can't make people grow. Rather, I can only create conditions conducive for their growth. What they do in that environment is their choice.

Similarly, I can't make a tree grow either. I can add fertilizer, water, and plant food, but no matter how much effort I exert, if the tree is unhealthy, it simply won't grow. And just like trees, not all people want to grow.

I remember one gentleman in particular. Let's call him Tony. No matter how much encouragement I gave him, he never seemed to be able to develop personally or professionally. I'm convinced he opposed personal growth.

One time I asked Tony if he read any books recently. He told me completely straight-faced that he'd just read *Who Cut the Cheese*. Of course, I wished he was referring to a parody of the number one bestseller *Who Moved My Cheese*. Unfortunately, he wasn't. I didn't know what made me more uncomfortable, the fact that he lied or the fact that he fumbled the real title. Looking back, I do have to chuckle a little about the title, but not about his lack of growth. My question to Tony wasn't out of the ordinary. I often ask people on my team what they're reading. I've found this question provides some soft accountability for them and me. If no one is asking us what we're reading, it's too easy to put it off. But even more rewarding than the question is the discussion that proceeds from their answer. We dialogue about our recent books and bring relevant truths into our specific situations within our organization.

Whenever I interact with my team members, I aim to be a catalyst for growth. First and foremost, I care about them. I'm not focused on changing them. Rather, I'm focused on growing them. Sometimes, being a catalyst is telling them what I'm doing. Other times, it's asking them a question. And still other times it's by offering them a tool or resource.

I remember a team member telling me he was going to be driving alone from West Palm Beach to Birmingham. During that time, I was half-way through a set of CDs that were incredibly thought-provoking. Always wanting to foster growth in others, I offered my teammate the ones I had just finished. Rather than accepting them or even kindly declining, he replied, "If I haven't learned it by now Scott, I guess I never will."

I was taken aback.

I didn't judge him, but I did feel a deep sadness for him. Knowing how resources have helped me improve spiritually and in relationships, business, skills, intelligence, and parenting, I grieved the fact that this man plateaued a long time long ago. His desire for growth was non-existent and he didn't value learning.

Needless to say, both of these men didn't stay long with our organization. They self-selected out because they didn't fit with our environment.

Please understand, we aren't looking for little robots. However, we desire people who believe the same things, but think different thoughts. For this to occur, people need to know what they believe. Unfortunately, many people don't know.

Books can help. They help fuel our beliefs. They stimulate our thinking and confront our prejudices. A good book, like a good conversation, will stick with you.

If you can't tell already, I'm a huge fan of books. Or maybe more accurately put, I'm a huge fan of certain books. Our organization developed some incentives to encourage our team members to read books that will help them grow and develop in their leadership skills.

Call it a maintenance strategy.

Because we value our people and their time, we pay them for the books they read. The team members only receive their book bonus when they give an oral report of what they learned and how they will apply these principles into their work and life.

Like I said, we're a little different.

Another topic we like to talk about is our E to E ratio—our education time compared to our entertainment time. I like entertainment just as much as anybody else, but healthy people digest entertainment *and* education. When we get unbalanced, we get unhealthy and unhealthy people can't lead themselves or others effectively.

A long time ago, I realized that we don't get what we want. We get who we are. People want lots of things. But simply wanting isn't enough. Becoming is.

The thing we have most control over is not other people, but ourselves. And by managing ourselves better, we increase our influence. That's why I work so hard on improving myself.

One of the ways I improve is by asking questions. Realistically, it would be hypocritical for me to ask everyone else questions and not myself. Although the questions I ask myself vary, I go back to my **Elite 8**.

1. What do I do best?
2. How can I do it better?
3. Who can I best serve doing it?
4. Of the things I currently do, what should I do more?
5. Of the things I currently do, what should I do less?
6. Of the things I currently do, what should I stop?
7. What should I start doing?
8. What am I missing?

Let me break them down one at a time and tell you why they're critical.

1. What do I do best?

Life is short. Why waste time doing things that don't provide a good return? Thanks to Marcus Buckingham's work on strengths (in books such as *Now Discover Your Strengths* and *StandOut),* we've been given permission to invest our time in endeavors we're good at. Effective people know what they're best at and focus on that activity. They delegate and release everything else.

2. How can I do it better?

This question differs ever so slightly from the first. It leaves room for potential to show up. Obviously, we don't want to jump in ignorantly, but at the same time we don't want to assume that we can't get better at something either. None of us has arrived, and we all have room to grow. This question prepares us to reach past our current position and into our future potential.

3. Who can I best serve doing it?

We've been given talents not to serve ourselves, but to serve others. We have no business getting good if we're not going to share that goodness with others. Identifying our tribe enables us to become more aware of the people around us who need our products and services. We can't help people if we don't know who *those people* are.

4. Of the things I currently do, what should I do more?

Once we take an inventory of everything we're doing, then—and only then—can we make informed decisions about what areas to focus on. Strategy and tactics emerge from this type of thinking. Everyone benefits when we invest more time in the few things that produce the best results.

5. Of the things I currently do, what should I do less?

When we recognize what we need to do more of, we naturally realize what we need to do less of, too. We're finite creatures and we can't keep piling on more and more without taking other things off our plate

6. What should I stop doing of the things I currently do?

Many people struggle with the decision to stop doing things. Why? The etymology of the English word *decide* gives us some clues. Decide comes from the Latin word *decidere*, which means "to cut off." And its cousin, the related Latin word *caedere*, means "to cut" or "to kill."

Think about all of our English words that end with "*cide*." Homicide, pesticide, insecticide, genocide, and suicide all come from this same Latin word *caedere*. So when we make a decision, we are literally "killing our options." We are cutting off the chance to remain open to other possibilities.

In a strange way, whenever we make a decision, we experience a type of loss. Dan Ariely, author of *Predictably Irrational*, explains the psychology behind indecision. "Closing a door on an option is experienced as a loss, and people are willing to pay a price to avoid the emotion of a loss."[36]

Odds are that to get better, you'll need to kill off something that you're currently doing. But first, you must get comfortable with the idea of experiencing a loss. Will your feeling of loss prevent you from getting better? Only you can *decide*.

7. What should I start doing?

Until we get comfortable killing off a current activity, we'll never be able to start a new one effectively. By killing off the old, we find the needed space for something new; something we should start doing. Both science and spirituality have taught this Universal Law directly and indirectly throughout the ages.

Spirituality teaches it one way. Omraam Mikhaël Aïvanhov, a Bulgarian Spiritual Master, observed that "a vacuum cannot exist in nature, but an empty space is immediately filled by something else."[37]

Similarly, science teaches that "nature abhors a vacuum." This view, called *horror vacui*, was proposed circa 485 BC by Greek physicist-philosopher Parmenides. He said, "A void, or rather a vacuum, in nature, cannot exist."[38]

Regardless of the angle, all of these sources point to one truth: two opposing elements cannot occupy the same space at the same time.

The Scriptures exhort us to "get rid of the old yeast so that you may be a new batch without yeast."[39] Another ancient writer posed this truth from a slightly different angle; "Can both fresh water and salt water flow from the same spring?"[40]

Simply put, you and I will continue to experience inner conflict until we stop doing what we know we shouldn't be doing. Only then can we create the space needed to improve, advance, and grow.

8. What am I missing?

I love this final question because it makes sure we stay in a teachable posture. We can't assume that we've figured out everything. No one has. Everyone has blind spots. Asking ourselves what we're missing prepares us to see those blind spots. Ignoring them won't make them go away. Of course, inviting a few Truth Tellers along the way will help us see ourselves even more clearly.

In this chapter, we looked at protecting our investment from a number of different angles. We observed how many organizations suffer from the post-hire curse, investing time and money in designing and building their team, but failing to invest in maintaining their team. We also explored the twelve dimensions of great managing and how most of them were directly tied to effective employee maintenance. And finally, we explored the Elite Eight questions that enable us to grow personally and professionally.

Although this fifth step in the Sweet Spot System™ is critical, we can't stop here. We have two more steps to take: 6: Maintain the Main Thing and 7: Give What You Can't Keep. Together, all seven proven steps help us create the life we want.

STEP 6:

MAINTAIN THE MAIN THING

Keep Your Vision within Sight at All Times

Did you ever notice how time lets us forget?

Although time may heal a broken heart, it also kills a perfect memory.

Here's what I mean. Because people forget what we say, vision must be communicated repeatedly. Life brings noise right along with it and our crystal-clear vision gets foggy pretty fast, even for us leaders—the ones communicating the vision.

Rick Warren tells us why. According to Amazon.com, Warren is "America's most influential spiritual leader" and the author of "the number one best-selling hardcover book of all time, *The Purpose Driven Life*." In his first book, Warren tells us how to help our people remember our vision through what he calls The Nehemiah Principle.

Evidently, thousands of years ago, the nation of Israel was rebuilding the walls around its city. Although the walls only took a brief fifty-two days to complete, about halfway through the project, the people became discouraged and wanted to quit. Fatigue, fear, and frustration set in. An intuitive leader, Nehemiah sensed that his people had lost sight of the vision. As a result, he recast the vision and the people saw their goal clearly again.

Warren extracted a principle from this historical account. The Nehemiah Principle declares, "Vision and purpose must be restated every twenty-six days" to keep the organization moving in the right direction.[41]

I've found this to be true in my own organization. No matter how many times we think we've said something, given enough time, that vision fades and we need to recast it again. Best-selling leadership author and communicator Andy Stanley explains the unique characteristics of vision. "Vision doesn't stick; it doesn't have natural adhesive. Instead, vision leaks."[42] Because vision leaks, we have a choice. We can ignore this reality or we can take action.

But what type of action?

Repetition helps, but people get bored with simple review. Although nothing replaces repetition, additional tools will help.

I keep a few principles on the forefront of my mind at all times. I call these The Five Lenses of Maintaining Vision. I've listed them here with brief descriptions.

1. Define the Vision

Legendary NFL coach Vince Lombardi didn't care if he insulted his players. Before the first practice of every season he would gather his team of world-class athletes, hold a football in the air, and say, "Gentleman, THIS is a football." He had an unwavering commitment for the basics, and winning five NFL championships proved to everyone that he and his team mastered the basics.

Lombardi *defined* the vision at every level, including the vision of every specific position of every specific player on every specific play. If his players couldn't *define* the vision, they couldn't *achieve* the vision.

Likewise, within our organization we've spent an enormous amount of time *defining* our vision. We don't leave it a mystery, nor do we allow our team the luxury of defining it themselves. When vision is left up to individuals to define, then it's always diluted—intentionally or unintentionally.

We've defined our vision as the GO2CO (The Go to Company) and we achieve this vision by disciplined people, disciplined thought, and disciplined action.[43] Although our vision is broad, we define it on many levels with very clear specificity. Here are the fourteen points.

Disciplined People

1. We recruit, hire, train, and advance the best people in the industry.
    - Hire the best, fire the rest
    - Aptitude, attitude, integrity
2. We are always learning (students).
3. The right people (doing the right things) are our biggest asset.
    - Strengths and weaknesses
4. Fewer people, working harder, making more, with a positive attitude.
    - We believe in "profitable" overtime
5. We surround ourselves with people who believe like we believe, but think different thoughts.

Disciplined Thought

6. Begin with the end in mind.
    - We maintain everything we install
7. Continue to learn and master all phases of our business.
    - Improve 1% each week = 52% each year
8. Everyone is a customer.
9. We are a team.
10. Believe in luck.
    - The harder I work, the luckier I get.

Disciplined Action

11. Take responsibility.
    - It's my job to make things better
12. Everything is marketing.
    - Marketing is the profitable getting and keeping of good customers
    - Uniforms, trucks, language, overall presentation

13. Sell! Sell! Sell!
    - Growth is our lifeline.
14. Keep order.
    - Chaos costs.

Develop the Vision

Once we *define* the vision, we must *develop* the vision. We choose new hires partially based upon their ability to flex and grow. Our rationale is simple. Because our organization is always developing, our people must be as well.

One of our recent developments around our vision is called the "Just Say It Once" initiative. We found we were spending far too much time repeating ourselves. This took its toll on our company, our customers, and our vendors. When defining vision, we need to be repetitive, but in the field—when carrying out directives—we need to be clear and concise.

Like point number fourteen of our vision explains, we must keep order because chaos costs. Our ineffective pattern of repeating ourselves was costing us time and money and something had to be done.

"Just Say it Once" helps fight against this tendency. It's code language for focusing intently the first time. We made the phrase part of our training and the entire organization knows exactly what we mean when we say it.

Because we designed and built our team with the right people who want to grow, we've been able to maintain it by *developing* vision initiatives like this one. No organization remains static, and neither can vision.

Imagine decades ago if a company's vision was to make the best VHS tapes. If that vision didn't change, that company would have died with old technology. The companies that survived the shifts from celluloid film to VHS tapes (and don't forget Betamax) to laser discs to

JUST SAY IT ONCE

With Each Other
Communicate effectively and set clear expectations

From the Customer
They only tell us once, and we make it happen

For the Vendor
Ask for what you need, when you need it,
from the vendor that can make it happen

JUST SAY IT ONCE

DVDs to Blu-Rays and digital downloads continued to develop their vision. Likewise, if we want to survive, our organization must continue to develop vision.

3. Drill the Vision

After defining the vision and continuing to develop the vision, it's time to drill the vision. Every good team realizes the importance of practicing together. Imagine driving to the big game to watch your favorite sports team play a tough opponent. Now imagine, on the way, you discover your team hasn't drilled together in more than six months. Would you still want to watch them? Probably not.

What about your team at work? Have you and your colleagues drilled as a team within the last six months? If not, why would anyone want to watch you, buy from you, or be associated with you?

Excellence doesn't happen by accident. One insightful boxer said, "Champions aren't made in the ring, they're revealed there." If you want your team to get better results, your team needs to get better by drilling the vision together.

Teams that don't want to drill together are typically teams that don't trust each other. Trust often erodes over time, even within the best organizations. A mistake here or a miscommunication there—multiplied over dozens of teammates—and in no time at all, a toxic environment emerges. Realizing this tendency, our organization developed what we call our "Social Contract". This initiative enables us to drill our vision and *build* trust rather than lose it. Our entire team makes this commitment to ourselves first and to each other second.

Our Social Contract serves us well because it positions us to serve each other. Each statement reflects our vision and pairs that vision with an action step. In a strategic way, it helps our team drill our vision on a daily basis.

When someone chooses to ignore the Social Contract, they know the consequences. Remember our friend, Jack, from chapter three? Jack was the guy who wanted to get out of the hot sun and sell because of his cancer, but then he snapped about not getting paid enough. Unfortunately, the Social Contract—the place where we drill our vision—became the context for Jack's downfall.

We eventually had to fire Jack. His departure resulted from his decision to break our Social Contract. Jack had a bad habit of initiating what we call "parking lot" chatter. You might know the habit. When guys show up before work, they talk around their trucks. No problem here. We encourage this type of relational connection. However, Jack viewed truck talk as his platform to gossip and complain about the organization.

Social Contract

I will...

- Represent the company's mission statement, core values, and social contract.
- Understand and fulfill my job description, expectations, and commitments.
- Inform the appropriate people ahead of time when I am convinced I cannot deliver on a promise.
- Trust other team members when there is a gap. (A gap is the difference between experience and expectation. When there is a gap, I can either believe the best or assume the worst.)
- Go directly to the appropriate team member if what I experience begins to erode my trust.
- Continue striving to be more effective every day in my area of responsibility.
- Make it my business to either know what has to be done or ask the right questions.
- Tell the appropriate people (those who are affected) when something goes wrong and how I will fix it.
- Come to a team member's defense when someone assumes the worst about him or her.
- Tell the truth when confronted about the gaps I've created.
- Confront because I trust.
- Not make the same mistake twice!

On the day we released him, he called one of our teammates, Debi Wysong, an incredibly derogatory word behind her back. I took his criticism incredibly personally. I told Jack, "Every time you criticize her, you criticize me." She's been charged with carrying out our vision.

Jack knows my approach to leadership. If teammates constructively criticize me in private, I will praise them. But if they criticize me or other teammates in public, I will fire them. Simply put, "Say it to me, I'll respect you. Say it about me, I'll fire you." Jack learned a difficult lesson that day—that our Social Contract is serious stuff and an integral part of our vision.

4. Distinguish the Vision

If the environment we designed, built, and maintained is effective, we should be able to quantify it and qualify it. A few of the ways we *distinguish* successful vision is observed via customer retention, client satisfaction, and increased referrals.

Effective vision must be measured with a clear grading scale. Imagine sports without a scoreboard. If we couldn't *distinguish* a clear winner or loser at the end of the game, no one would show up to watch.

It's the same thing with companies. When teammates can't tell how to put a "W" on the board, they feel frustrated. And if left unchecked, they'll eventually stop showing up altogether.

We created a way to distinguish successful vision through an initiative called "I Love My Job," coined by teammate Mike VanBrocklin. We printed "I Love My Job" on special hats and we only award them under one condition. Teammates who want these hats need to explain why they love their job with specific, measurable examples.

If employees are wearing one of these hats, naturally we know that customers and vendors are going to ask why they love their job. Because of this, we'd like our teammates to be equipped ahead of time. You'd be surprised how a simple hat has prepared our people to *distinguish* our vision with more clarity and confidence. In addition, it's helped spread the word about the type of environment we're designing, building, and maintaining.

We would have never guessed that a simple hat initiative would become a major marketing tool, too, but it has. And because we now have a long list of measurable wins from the testimonies of our teammates, they're more excited and empowered. Clear and *distinguishable* vision motivates everyone involved.

5. Demonstrate the Vision

Logically, the final lens is to *demonstrate* the vision. Especially in a tough economy, we must embody our vision every day, at all times. Our team knows competition is tough and our customers have many other options besides us. Every job serves as another opportunity to prove our competence and win customer loyalty. We can work congruently and live out our vision or we can work hypocritically and bury it. Every teammate, every minute of the day, encounters this choice.

Based upon this realization, our organization created a small initiative called "Because the Customer". Here's the language.

Because the Customer:

- Has a need, we have a job to do!
- Has a choice, we must be the better choice!
- Has sensibilities, we must be considerate!
- Has an urgency, we must be quick!
- Has high expectations, we must excel!
- Is unique, we must be flexible!
- Is a customer, we exist!

Each of these statements reflects the critical need for us to *demonstrate* our vision. Our "Because the Customer" initiative puts our customers exactly where they belong: first place. And if we demonstrate our vision effectively, this initiative will put us exactly where we'd like to be: first choice.

We've taken six of the proven steps in The Sweet Spot System™ and now we only have one more step to take. Regrettably, most organizations make the fatal flaw of skipping this final step. But beware! Missing this step is a critical misstep. To leave a lasting legacy we must take step seven and Give What We Can't Keep.

STEP 7:

GIVE WHAT YOU CAN'T KEEP

Legacies are Maintained by Investing in Others

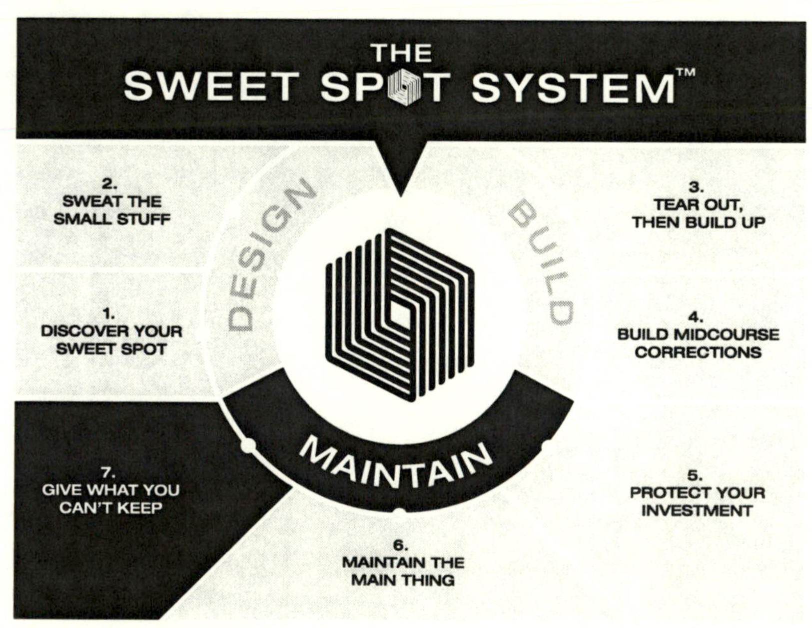

I took my son, Andrew, to his first property closing when he was only 12 years old. Since then, I've taken him to about a half dozen more. Some of the other attendees were five times his age—most of them experts in their respective field. Onlookers might classify my choice as cruel and unusual punishment. Who would subject a child to what might appear as a boring meeting with a CPA and an attorney?

But because I'm his father, I had a bigger reason.

When I was 12 years old, my dad pulled me out of class to join him at a few ministerial meetings. The other attendees *seemed* ten times my age—most of them experts in their respective field. But he didn't just subject his child to a boring meeting with pastors and ministry leaders.

Because he's my father, he had a bigger reason, too.

Time is short. Legacies are forever.

My father understood that legacies are maintained by investing in others. Rather than a shortsighted perspective for my happiness, he had a long-term vision for my growth. He knew that pouring into me certain ideas and experiences would stretch me and expose me to new types of thinking. He believed specific situations would shape who I am, so he planted within me an environment conducive to my growth.

My dad has a healthy perspective of life…and death, for that matter. He knew he wouldn't always be around. Some might call this perspective morbid. I call it realistic.

When we live like we're *never* going to die, we design our lives so they only benefit us. But when we live *knowing* we're going to die, we design our lives for the benefit of others, too. Educator Elton Trueblood understood the importance of investing in the next generation. He said, "We have made at least a start in discovering the meaning in human life when we plant shade trees under which we know full well we will never sit."

My father understood this common truth in an uncommon way. As a result, he knew his impact wouldn't pass when he passed. He grew those around him and his legacy manifested itself in people, not possessions.

Martyred missionary Jim Elliott said, "He is no fool who gives what he cannot keep to gain what he cannot lose." Those of us who fully integrate The Sweet Spot System™ give what we can't keep: our very lives. Sometimes we need to invest our time, sometimes our trust, and sometimes our truth. Regardless, we pour into others because we value them and the legacy we deposit within them. In my specific story, step number seven became the greatest magnifier of my success. I didn't set out to *do great* or *be great.* Instead, I invested greatly in others and slowly over time, my work *became great* because of the people around me.

But that's jumping ahead. I must begin the story surrounding step seven right back where we first started, in—of all places—my pickup truck.

"If you're enjoying any success in your life, it's because someone has gone before you, sacrificed, and paid the price."

The voice coming through the stereo jolted me and the meaning behind the words ripped straight through my soul. Tears pooled up in my eyes and the road in front of me turned blurry fairly fast. If I didn't pull over to the side of the road, I knew I might wreck my pickup. Unbeknownst to the friend who let me borrow this cassette teaching called *Statements of Success*, the content reflected an uncanny relevance to my situation.

Moments later I pulled over safely, turned off the ignition, and wept. Three names immediately came to mind.

My Dad.

Greg Lawrence.

Steve Addison.

The success in my life at that point was a direct result of these three men who went before me, sacrificed, and paid the price. Each invested something unique.

My Dad: Invested Time

To supplement his income while serving as a preacher, my dad opened a store called *The Junk Shop* when I was still quite young. The store brought in extra money that helped our family make it through some of those lean years. He'd find all kinds of items—from high-end kitchen cabinets to bike frames that needed to be fixed up. He'd purchase these items from Pennsylvania to New York.

During one season, my dad and I bought and raised two Hereford calves. His commitment for us to thrive made us think creatively. He'd buy the food for the calves and I'd clean their stalls.

We shared ownership until the day we received a mini bike on consignment. I begged my dad to let me sell him my calf so I could purchase the mini bike. He eventually agreed, and I rode the life out of that bike. After it died, I'd fix it back up again and head out for some more adventure.

My dad taught me a lesson in appreciation and depreciation. He said, "Every day you own the bike, it will be worth less. But every day you own the calf, it will be worth more." Although I understood that lesson intellectually, I wasn't quite ready to apply it.

I learned many things from working with my dad in *The Junk Shop*—like how to buy, sell, price, and negotiate. I learned how to work with my hands and how to work with people. Those lessons set me in a direction and they set me up for success. My dad didn't consider the *time* he spent with me a waste, but rather an investment in his legacy and my potential.

Greg Lawrence: Invested Trust

A couple years after I returned to Florida from New York, I received a call from a distressed friend and fellow landscaper, Greg Lawrence. He had recently left his landscaping business to go into the ministry full time. Rather than selling the landscaping organization, he entrusted it to three good-natured technicians who lacked business savvy. Despite the best intentions and some working capital, the company teetered on bankruptcy. "Scottie, I know you can help me," he pleaded. "I don't have much left. I'll give you my assets and my debt. I just want my name to be cleared so I can move on and focus on my new calling."

When I received his phone call, I was in no position to take on a business because I had no capital. If I wanted to keep Greg's business afloat, I'd have to leave my job and take a cut in salary. Besides, I had a young family to care for and a small house to manage.

Still, in spite of all the reasons not to acquire Greg's business I felt incredibly honored by his phone call. He believed in me at a time when I didn't believe in myself.

Usually, we're the last to see our own potential and in this particular situation, Greg saw mine long before I did. Even though he was in a tough situation, Greg intuitively knew my sweet spot was business and his sweet spot was ministry.

And so, by Greg handing over his checkbook, he also handed over his trust. His business became the first of fourteen I'd eventually acquire. Greg didn't consider the *trust* he gifted me a waste, but rather an investment in his legacy and my potential.

Steve Addison: Invested Truth

I entered Hobe Sound Bible College in need of a mentor. Lucky for me, Steve Addison, the dean of men, decided to be one for me. Each time we met, he invested his heart. As time marched on, his investment in me went beyond the role of dean.

Steve became my Truth Teller. If I needed to purchase property, he'd offer his perspective. If I needed to make a relational decision, he'd offer his insight. But more than that, Steve's truth took shape. He didn't sit still. Rather, he took an active role within my life.

Steve not only embodied truth, but when he found it, he made sure to share it, including the cassette teaching that I listened to in my truck in that day. At that point in my life, I was only slightly familiar with speaker John Maxwell. A few years before that, my father had given me one of his books as a Christmas present: *Developing the Leader within You*. Listening to John Maxwell that day in my truck, I knew I needed to get more of this type of truth. Little did I know how that one cassette would change my life and the lives of hundreds of thousands around the world.

Following the pattern, Steve didn't consider the *truth* he shared with me a waste, but rather an investment in his legacy and my potential.

Upon hearing the teaching in the truck that day, I immediately made three separate calls: one to my dad, one to Greg, and one to Steve. I thanked each of them separately for the investment they made in me through the years and I expressed appreciation for the legacy they built within me.

A few days later, I knew what I needed to do. I needed to share this teaching with others: family members, friends, colleagues, vendors, and everyone else I ran into. I called up the John Maxwell Company and a woman named Winnie answered. She was not only extremely competent, but also incredibly kind. I placed my first order for fifty cassette tapes, and so began our friendship. During the next few months, anytime I wanted to invest in others, I'd call up Winnie and order more of those cassettes called *MIC (Maximum Impact Club) Lessons*. Later, I discovered Winnie was the wife of Doug Carter, the president of EQUIP Leadership Inc., a non-profit global leadership development organization founded by John Maxwell.

Thinking back, Winnie must have been either scared or impressed by the number of cassettes I ordered. My monthly purchases certainly outpaced my pay grade. Regardless, Winnie told her husband Doug about a landscaper from Florida who invested in everyone he met by leveraging John Maxwell's leadership lessons on cassette tape.

John's content on leadership lit a fire inside me. I knew I could improve my organization if I improved my people and I knew I could improve my people if I improved myself. I took responsibility for the gaps in my life and became a serious student of personal growth. More than simply buying leadership resources, I also applied the principles and integrated the practices within my life. In a short amount of time, my organization grew exponentially. I even purchased John's materials for leaders within my church and began training them on the weekends.

A few months later, Doug Carter invited me to the first public conference in the brand new sanctuary at Christ Fellowship Church in West Palm Beach, Florida. Evidently, John Maxwell was giving a seminar on his new book at the time, *The 21 Irrefutable Laws of Leadership*. Doug explained that at the event John would host a private dinner for a couple dozen leaders. Without hesitation I agreed to go. I wanted to meet the man who invested in me at a distance through his books and lectures.

The content that day didn't disappoint. John was at the top of his game, except I could tell for him this was no game. He lived and breathed his materials. He wasn't sharing his lectures, he was sharing his *life*.

A few years later, I saw John at a business breakfast. When the opportunity came for me to grab a few moments with him, I knew I needed to somehow repay this teacher who had helped me discover the tools I was using to create my legacy.

"Mr. Maxwell," I spoke, fumbling for the correct words. "You don't know me, but I am deeply indebted to you," I continued, trying to find my authentic voice in real time. "My name is Scott Fay, and your materials have helped me embrace my purpose and my passion. I'm now developing the people within my organization and I want to repay you. I'm just an irrigation contractor, but I serve some of the world's top entertainers and athletes. Please let me take care of your landscape irrigation needs for life. It won't cost you a dime, and I'll personally ensure that you have the best quality and care."

With those words I laid out my perfect plan. What else could John say, except "Yes!"

But unfortunately, he said, "No."

John looked at me and smiled sincerely. "Well, Scott, that's very generous of you. I'm thrilled that my materials are helping you get better results within your life and your organization. However, I can't accept. I live in a condominium and all my landscaping needs are already cared for. But thanks for your offer."

And with that unfortunate news our conversation ended naturally, but abruptly. What else could either of us say?

I left the seminar that day excited for everything I learned, but I was also somewhat disappointed. Although I connected with John Maxwell again, I didn't get to add value to his life.

Nonetheless, as time marched on, I kept leading my organization and investing in myself and my teams. We posted better numbers each consecutive year.

A while later, I heard about a private fundraiser John Maxwell was doing for Hobe Sound Bible College. The investment was $5,000 per ticket. Without hesitation I purchased two, despite being ridiculed by several different people close to me.

I brought a colleague with me that sunny day in Florida. I wanted him to learn and grow just like I had. Again, the session that day stretched me. And again, I cornered John on a break.

"Hi, John," I started out again. "Scott Fay here. I hear you have a new house. I know I made this offer to you a couple years back, but I really want to repay you for the investment you've made in me. Please let me take care of all your landscaping needs for life."

Prepared for another strikeout, thankfully Providence allowed me to hit a grand slam. John and his wife, Margaret, had since moved out of their condominium into a beautiful home surrounded by water on three sides. According to him, they were in between landscapers and my offer came at just the right time. To my delight, he accepted.

At their earliest convenience, I met him and Margaret at their house and enjoyed a tour of their property. I made detailed notes of every feature, plant, and tree they wanted. John kept assuring me he'd pay full price for my services. After rejecting his generosity a half dozen times, John revealed how he would repay me.

"Scott, I'd be happy to mentor you. It's one way to repay you for your services. Here's my assistant's phone number," he said, handing me a card. "Just call Linda and she'll set us up with an appointment."

I later discovered that, despite his complex schedule and international speaking tour, John chose a few people to mentor each year.

By taking Linda's card, I felt like I'd just been handed a million dollars. I showed up that day simply to give back to the man who invested in me through his books and lectures. And now, here he had just offered to personally mentor me.

"John…I…umm…I…I don't know what to say," the words stumbled out of my mouth. "Except that…I guess you might just be the toughest person to get even with," I jested.

John looked at me with a warm smile and exclaimed, "Keep trying, baby. Keep trying." And with that humorous exchange, we both laughed and continued the tour around his property.

That sunny day in Florida, my relationship with John Maxwell began. Linda's call finally came and so did my first mentoring session. I came fully prepared and took copious notes.

Over the years, our friendship grew beyond my wildest imagination. However, no one could have ever predicted what would happen next. Because of a funeral home, a sand bar, and a couple of guys in their underwear, I played a role in helping the number one leadership guru in the world create a significant legacy piece and the fastest-growing speaking, coaching, and training team. Currently, we have a few thousand coaches in nearly 100 countries, and we're not about to stop growing. Here's the backstory behind John's legacy piece.

I met Paul Martinelli in, of all places, a funeral home. You've heard about being in the right place at the right time? For Paul Martinelli, there is no right place or right time. Instead, according to him, we *make* it the right time and place by taking the right action. And that's just what Paul did.

He invited me to be part of his mastermind group and I agreed. An eclectic group of men, we represented a variety of disciplines from janitorial to insurance, from contracting to landscaping. One topic bound us together: personal growth. Each of us had a passion to grow ourselves and our teams. We invested our time, trust, and truth in other people for their benefit and not ours.

This particular mastermind group evolved into a unique band of brothers committed to bringing the best in personal growth to our region. We designed seminars, mastermind groups, training experiences, and coaching packages. Paul, the master navigator, developed his skills so well that he eventually partnered with a prominent personal growth expert and subsequently designed structures and systems for him. He helped that particular teacher transition from developing content to instead designing legacy.

He and Paul eventually parted ways on good terms, but Paul knew he had discovered something truly unique. Paul's destiny centered on helping select people create powerful legacies.

Eventually, Paul and I chatted about my mentor, John Maxwell. We both knew the potential of John's legacy. With credibility in multiple sectors—entertainment, government, education, business, and faith—John's footprint affected the entire world already. His non-profit company, Equip, trained more than 5 million leaders in more than 150 countries. Still, Paul knew John could reach more if he created a team to spread his legacy.

Unfortunately, John gets pitched multiple times a month on multiple topics. We certainly didn't want to be like everyone else by pitching to John. Still, we knew he needed to hear the big vision in a big way if he'd accept. And so we prepared.

Always wanting to give back to John for his investment in me, I constantly looked for unique ways to bless this mentor of mine who travels the world teaching leadership principles to presidents, professional athletes, and pastors. One particular opportunity stemmed from an invitation for a rare luncheon on a friend's yacht.

"John, I'd love to set up a special lunch for you," I explained. My good friend, Angelo Schiralli and his son Branden, have a gorgeous yacht. Why don't I have him pick us up, right from your dock, and we can cruise up and down the channel while enjoying a wonderful lunch? You'll love it."

Always up for a little adventure, John agreed.

A couple weeks later, I stood on John's dock waiting for my friend to pick us up. Those who know John Maxwell know he can't even spell the word P-A-T-I-E-N-C-E. After about five minutes, John got restless and I got nervous. Grasping for topics to ease the situation, I went for one that might pique his interest: legacy.

Maxwell and *legacy* are two words intertwined together. He addresses this subject in several of his best-selling books. For example, in *The 21 Irrefutable Laws of Leadership,* he defines the Law of Legacy by stating that a leader's lasting value is measured by succession. Those who know John know that he enjoys *writing* on legacy and, more importantly, *living out* his legacy.

"John, please grab a seat here on the dock. I have something to tell you." My very suggestion seemed to offer him some solace from the somewhat tense situation. "I need to tell you about my friend, Paul Martinelli. I believe he could really help you expand your legacy."

And so, for the next twenty minutes I explained about Paul's ability to create systems and structures around content and principles. I shared how he helped other personal growth experts extend their reach. Nearing the end of my spiel, I asked John, "So, what do you think?"

"Well, Scott, tell Paul to put together a proposal and send it to my assistant, Linda," he responded rather woodenly. Evidently, John had even been pitched on this topic before. A few business-minded individuals approached John over the years about starting his own coaching company. Although potentially rewarding, an endeavor like this one contained many liabilities as well, including risking his 40-year reputation in the industry with other coaches he didn't even know.

Just then, I received a phone call from my business partner, Tom Balling. He explained that their yacht had become stuck on a sandbar in the channel. My friends had to strip down to their boxers and push the boat off the sandbar to get it moving again. He instructed John and me to hop in our vehicles and meet him at another dock so we could begin our lunch excursion.

With that news, I hung up the phone, ended the chat about Paul, and headed down to the next dock ready for our afternoon adventure.

With the green light from John, Paul put the finishing touches on his proposal a couple weeks later. Obviously in his sweet spot, Paul utilized several other players when drafting the document. He incorporated legal protocol, financial data, and legacy language. However, despite all our work, I still had to deliver the document to John. Unfortunately, John has layers of people between himself and new initiatives. He is committed to staying in his sweet spot, regardless of many good opportunities. I knew this particular proposal would be difficult to get in front of him. Besides, he instructed me to go through Linda, so I did.

Sort of.

"Hi, Linda. It's Scott," I said rather strategically. "Hey, thanks for taking my phone call. John asked me to pass on a proposal to you," I explained. "I have three copies for you right here with me."

"Yes, thanks Scott," she responded. "Just put them in the mail and I will make sure John sees them," she instructed.

"Oh, I will," I assured her. "But I have to ask; if I happen to see John, can I give him one of the copies?" I questioned.

"Scott, just put them in the mail and I will make sure he gets them," she held her ground firmly.

"Of course," I responded respectfully. "I'll overnight them to you. But if I just happen to see John, can I give him one of the copies?" I asked one final time.

After a long pause on the phone, Linda eventually replied. "Fine, Scott. If you see John, you may give him one of the copies."

"Thanks, Linda. You're the best," I said, hanging up the phone.

Then I stepped out of my pickup truck and onto John's property. Parked outside his driveway, I had designed my schedule intent on "just happening" to see John that day. As I entered his backyard, I saw a familiar site: John swimming laps in his Infinity pool, complete with a customized underwater sound system. Unfortunately for me, John's snorkel ensured that he wouldn't be coming up for air for quite some time.

By sticking my hand into the pool, John must have seen me. Content to take a short break, he eventually surfaced."Hey, Scott," he welcomed me warmly. "What's up?"

"Hi, John," I greeted back. "I was near the area so I wanted to drop off Paul's proposal."

"Sure, Scott. Just put it over there on the table," he instructed.

"Of course, John. By the way, would you have some time so Paul and I can sit down and discuss the proposal with you?" I inquired.

"I'm afraid not, Scott," he shared. "I'm not even golfing now. I'm working on my next book and not doing any new projects."

"OK, John," I said sincerely. "I understand. Well, I don't want to hold you up from your exercise. But one last thing. Your message from Sunday…"

"Yes," John briefly interrupted. "What is it?"

"John, I gotta tell you. That message really touched me," I shared. "There's a few things I'm going through, John. And…well, it really spoke to me on multiple levels."

"Really?" John said. After another moment John communicated an idea. "Tell you what, Scott. Call Linda and set up a lunch with me for later this week. I'd love to hear what's going on in your life."

John's care was obvious and his concern for me—edifying. He always puts others first.

"I'd love to meet for lunch," I answered. "But John, just one more thing" I posed.

"Yes, Scott?""At the end of our lunch, may I invite Paul to stop in for the last ten minutes?" I asked, respectfully.

John paused for an extended period.

"Scott, as long as we're getting together to talk about you." His reply contained a directive, not a question.

"Absolutely, John," I submitted.

And with that exchange, the plan was set. During the course of the next few months, John and his team met with Paul and me. Together, we crafted what would become The John Maxwell Team.[44] None of us could have predicted the legacy that would emerge from this team, including YouthMax—a curriculum we taught to more than 100,000 teens around the world. This four-fold content centered on leadership issues related to failing forward, self-esteem, anti-bullying, and personal character. Thousands of lives were changed, including those of several teens who chose life rather than suicide.

One single cassette program called *Statements of Success* shared by Steve Addison and, years later, nearly 100 countries now have

John Maxwell-certified speakers, coaches, and trainers. My life is a living reflection of others who invested in me—people like Steve, Greg, John, and my dad.

One simple thought uttered from that cassette propelled me to start living in light of my legacy. I'll never forget it. "If you're enjoying any success in your life, it's because someone has gone before you, sacrificed, and paid the price."

And so it is with you, too.

Are you enjoying any success?

Who's gone before you, sacrificed, and paid the price?

Remember: because they invested in you, you are now part of their legacy.

A man once asked, "When is the best time to plant a tree?"

His friend replied automatically, "Twenty years ago."

Regretfully, he realized he missed that particular goal.

"Well, when's the second best time?" he inquired again.

"Today," his friend wisely replied.

And so it is with legacies; yours and mine alike. If you've never intentionally started maintaining your legacy, today is the second best time to begin.

AFTERWORD: KEEP YOUR FORK

"During his long life, Roy Rood treated people like trees. He gave them the right environment, plenty of nourishment, and watched something beautiful grow."[45]

These words concluded a warmhearted article in *The Palm Beach Post,* affirming the life of Roy Rood. If you remember back a few chapters, Roy was the former vendor of mine who hired me back to pull weeds for $8.50 an hour. He's also the same man whose company I'd eventually purchase years later. (Turns out the comment he told me twenty years prior— *"And if you're willing to go through the process, the table has something to special to bring to you"*—was both prophetic and educational.

Roy discovered his sweet spot and everyone knew it—his friends, his family, and even the President of the United States! In 1987, his company won the coveted $3 million contract to landscape The Gardens Mall in Palm Beach Gardens. The contract required 1,000 queen palms, 1,000 Washingtonian palms, 7,500 cocoplum shrubs, and five miles of edging plants around the mall property. When his workers couldn't locate the 165 Canary Island date palms required for the job, Roy himself traveled around the state, buying palms out of homeowners' yards. His work was so impressive that he won an award for The Gardens Mall landscape, handed to him on the White House lawn by then-first lady Barbara Bush.

Although he started with nothing but hand tools—a wheelbarrow, shovels, and a crosscut saw—he built Rood Landscape into a multimillion-dollar enterprise. Born in a small Florida town, in a rural area north of Indiantown Road that is now Jupiter Farms, he graduated from Jupiter High School in 1936. When Mr. Rood was only a child, his father was killed in a car crash and community members helped raise Mr. Rood and his ten siblings.[46] He then spent much of the rest of his life showing his gratitude through good deeds.

He served his country in World War II and he served his community the rest of his life. He became a founding member of Jupiter Christian School in 1963, organized the first Kiwanis Club and Girl Scouts troop in Jupiter, started the Jupiter/Tequesta Athletic Association, founded the American Legion Post in Jupiter and helped launch Jupiter's first fire department.

Why conclude my first book with an afterword focused on Roy Rood? Great question. Here's the answer.

In our disposable, instant access, microwavable, downloadable, and fast-paced world, Roy Rood stood out. He *discovered* his sweet spot and just as important, he *stayed* in that sweet spot. Look around. Recent history provides examples of people who *stayed* in their sweet spot: Billy Graham, Steve Jobs, and Mother Theresa. Recent history also reveals those who left their sweet spot: Oprah Winfrey, Brett Favre, and Tiger Woods.

You be the judge.

What life do you want to create?

What legacy do you want to leave?

Roy Rood made his decision ahead of time.

He embodied all seven steps in The Sweet Spot System™. He designed, built, and maintained the life he wanted and created an environment conducive to growing himself and those around him. Rood Institute—a leadership development initiative—was just one expression his conducive environment. More than 60 local companies were born out of the Institute.

At Roy's funeral on October 22, 2011, one of the last speakers concluded the service by sharing a word picture I often think about. Evidently, Roy's mother would generously clean up the dishes at the conclusion of every meal. Each person would place their spoons and knives on their dirty plates and pass them to her. While collecting them, she'd make a very important announcement. *"Keep your fork,"* she'd say. "The best is yet to come. I'm bringing dessert."

Reflecting upon Roy Rood, the speaker told us, *"Keep your fork.* Roy may be gone, but his legacy still lives on. The best is yet to come."

And so it is with both you and me. If we discover our sweet spot and live within that sweet spot, our friends and family should *keep their forks,* too.

Our best is yet to come.

DISCUSSION QUESTIONS

Phase 1: Design Your Leadership Environment

Step 1: Discover Your Sweet Spot
Design with the End in Mind

1. What is required of me?
2. What yields the highest return?
3. What creates the greatest reward?
4. What makes me laugh?
5. What makes me sing?
6. What makes me cry?
7. What's different about what makes me laugh, sing, and cry?

Step 2: Sweat the Small Stuff
The Devils are in the Design

1. Reread the five Devil Destroyers and then answer these questions.

2. What am I accepting as normal that I should reject?

3. What are my beliefs based on; assumption or fact?

4. How could I get the best results possible?

5. Of all the things I'm currently doing, what should I change?

6. What Design Devils need to be redesigned within my life or organization?

Phase 2: Build Your Leadership Environment

Step 3: Tear Out, Then Build Up
Prepare the Ground for Your Dream to Take Root

1. What are the things in my life that could be defined as weeds?

2. What are the good or bad things in my life that are taking time and energy away from the best things?

3. What agendas or expectations are other people trying to place within my life?

4. What nonessential things have I allowed to take up space within my life?

Step 4: Build Midcourse Corrections
Blessed are the Flexible for They Shall Not Break

1. How do I evaluate my original plan based upon the current situations in my life?

2. What is my system to correct the problem?

3. How do I respond to unexpected change?

4. How do I daily connect with my Purpose, Passion, and Plan?

5. How do I daily change my experience into insight?

Phase 3: Maintain Your Leadership Environment

Step 5: Protect Your Investment
Poor Maintenance Costs You More in the Long Run

1. How am I helping the people around me grow?

2. How am I setting the example?

3. How does my growth environment show up in my datebook and my checkbook?

4. List the most recent leadership book, article, podcast, or seminar I've read, listened to, or attended.

Step 6: Maintain the Main Thing
Keep Your Vision within Sight at All Times

1. How have I drilled with my team within the last six months?

2. My core values, personally and professionally are:

3. I would define my personal social contract as:

4. Do those closest to me reflect my core values and social contract? Why or why not?

Step 7: Give What You Can't Keep
Legacies are Maintained by Investing in Others

1. What am I doing to live beyond myself?

2. Who am I pouring myself into?

3. How will I be remembered?

ENDNOTES

1 "How to Choose the Right Cologne for Your Lifestyle," *Esquire*, November 17, 2012," http://www.esquire.com/style/grooming/mens-cologne-reviews-0709#slide-1", accessed October 26, 2012

2 Peter Gosling, "Fascinating Tree Seed Facts", *The Tree Seed Consultant*, http://www.treeseedconsultant.co.uk/average-seeds-per-tree.html, accessed July 20, 2012.

3 Michael Hyatt, "An Interview with Dan Cathy", http://michaelhyatt.com/an-interview-with-dan-cathy.html, accessed July 22, 2012.

4 L. P. Jacks, *Education through Recreation* (New York: Harper & Brothers, 1932), 1.

5 Professor Francis J. Aguilar and Richard G. Hamermesh and RA Caroline Brainard, "General Electric: 1984" (HBS Case No. 385-315), http://www.shkaminski.com/Classes/Readings/GE-Welch.htm, accessed August 20, 2012.

6 Noel Tichy and Ram Charan, "Speed, Simplicity, Self-Confidence: An Interview with Jack Welch," *Harvard Business Review*, September-October 1989, http://www.shkaminski.com/Classes/Readings/GE-Welch.htm, accessed August 20, 2012.

7 Thomas A. Stewart, Ann Harrington, and Maura Griffin Solovar, "America's Most Admired Companies: Why Leadership Matters," Fortune, March 2, 1998, http://money.cnn.com/magazines/fortune/fortune_archive/1998/03/02/238547/index.htm, accessed August 20, 2012.

8 GE, http://www.ge.com/company/history/bios/john_welch.html, accessed September 1, 2012.

9 Geoffrey Colvin, "What makes GE great?" *Fortune*, February 22, 2006, http://money.cnn.com/2006/02/21/magazines/fortune/mostadmired_fortune_ge/index.htm, accessed September 2, 2012

10 Kate Dubose, "Most Common Resume Lies," Fortune, May 23, 2006, http://www.forbes.com/2006/05/20/resume-lies-work_cx_kdt_06work_0523lies.html, assessed April 11, 2013.
11 Howard Schultz and JoAnne Gordon, *Onward*, (New York, Rodale Books, 2011).
12 Anne Fisher, "How Starbucks got its groove back," *Fortune*, March 24, 2011, http://management.fortune.cnn.com/2011/03/24/how-starbucks-got-its-groove-back/, accessed September 23, 2012
13 Alice in Wonderland Site, "Alice in Wonderland Quotes," http://www.alice-in-wonderland.net/books/alice-in-wonderland-quotes.html, accessed July 27, 2012.
14 Today this wouldn't be so easy. Jeffy has since grown up into Jeff—a fairly muscular football player. On this day, he was a small kid who loved adventure.
15 Dictionary.com, http://dictionary.reference.com/browse/midcourse+correction, accessed November 2, 2012.
16 More on Captain Sully found in *The Deeper Path*. Kary Oberbrunner, (Grand Rapids, Baker Books, 2013).
17 Chesley Sullenberger, *Highest Duty* (New York: HarperCollins, 2009).
18 "US Airways Flight 1549 Initial Report" (press release), *US Airways*, January 15, 2009.
19 Katie Couric, "Capt. Sully Worried About Airline Industry," *CBS News*, June 12, 2009, http://www.cbsnews.com/2100-18563_162-4791429.html, accessed July 22, 2012.
20 Robert Kolker, "'My Aircraft': Why Sully may be the last of his kind," *New York Magazine*, February 1, 2009, http://nymag.com/news/features/53788/.
21 Melina Liu. "Architectural White Elephants: Beijing, London, and the Post-Olympics Curse," *The Daily Beast*, August 14, 2012, http://www.thedailybeast.com/articles/2012/08/14/architectural-white-elephants-beijing-london-and-the-post-olympics-curse.html, accessed December 25, 2012.
22 Elena Becatoros. "Athens Olympics Venues In Decay 8 Years After 2004 Games," *The Huffington Post*, August 3, 2012, http://www.huffingtonpost.com/2012/08/03/athens-olympics-venues-photos-abandoned_n_1739264.html, accessed December 25, 2012.
23 Ibid.
24 Helena Smith." Athens 2004 Olympics: what happened after the athletes went home," *The Guardian*, May 9, 2012, http://www.guardian.co.uk/sport/2012/may/09/athens-2004-olympics-athletes-home, accessed December 25, 2012.
25 Ibid
26 Ibid.
27 Ibid.
28 "General and Specific Purpose of Job Description," Management Study Guide, http://www.managementstudyguide.com/job-description-purpose.htm, accessed December 25, 2012.
29 Rod Wagner and James K. Hartler, 12: The Elements of Great Managing (Washington D.C.: Gallup Press, 2006).
30 Isaiah 50:4

31 Anti-perform is a term I use. It simply blends the prefix *anti* with the word *perform*. It means against or opposed to performing.
32 Josh Bersin. "It's Not the CEO, It's the Leadership Strategy that Matters," *Forbes*, http://www.forbes.com/sites/joshbersin/2012/07/30/its-not-the-ceo-its-the-leadership-strategy-that-matters/2/, accessed December 26, 2012
33 Patricia O'Connell, "How Companies Develop Great Leaders," *Businessweek*, February 16, 2010, http://www.businessweek.com/stories/2010-02-16/how-companies-develop-great-leadersbusinessweek-business-news-stock-market-and-financial-advice, accessed December 26, 2012.
34 Patricia O'Connell, "How Companies Develop Great Leaders," *Businessweek*, February 16, 2010, http://www.businessweek.com/stories/2010-02-16/how-companies-develop-great-leadersbusinessweek-business-news-stock-market-and-financial-advice, accessed December 26, 2012.
35 Susan Scott, Fierce Conversations, (New York, Berkley Trade, 2004)
36 Dan Ariely, *Predictably Irrational* (New York: Harper Collins, 2008)
37 Renford, *The Laws of Material Workbook* (Memphis: IAMPress, 2006)
38 *Encyclopedia of Human Thermodynamics*, http://www.eoht.info/page/Nature+abhors+a+vacuum, accessed December 29, 2012.
39 1 Corinthians 5:7
40 James 3:11
41 Rick Warren, *The Purpose Driven Church* (Grand Rapids: Zondervan, 1995).
42 Andy Stanley, Vision Leaks, *Christianity Today*, 2004 Winter, http://www.christianitytoday.com/le/2004/winter/19.68.html, accessed December 29, 2012
43 Thanks to Jim Collins for the "disciplined" inspiration found in his insightful book, *Good to Great*
44 http://www.johnmaxwellgroup.com
45 Barbara Marshall, An appreciation of the remarkable Roy Rood," *The Palm Beach Post*, October 15, 2011, http://www.palmbeachpost.com/news/news/an-appreciation-of-the-remarkable-roy-rood/nLyqq/, accessed January 8, 2012.
46 Jason Schultz, "Pioneer Roy Rood helped landscape much of northern Palm Beach County," *The Palm Beach Post*, October 15, 2011, http://www.palmbeachpost.com/news/social-networking/obituary-pioneer-roy-rood-helped-landscape-much-of/nLyjz/, accessed January 8, 2012.

ABOUT THE AUTHOR

Scott Fay is a student, practitioner, and teacher of leadership and business practices. His content is hewn from the experience of acquiring more than a dozen failing landscape businesses and rolling them into two industryleading organizations, building a commercial real estate portfolio, and partnering with the John C. Maxwell Certification Program. A speaker, trainer, and author committed to growing himself and the people around him, Scott is passionate about creating effective leadership *environments.*

CPSIA information can be obtained at www.ICGtesting.com
Printed in the USA
LVOW13s1401151113

361473LV00003B/18/P